BUILDING ᴬᴺARK

D1008108

BUILDING AN ARK

TOOLS FOR THE PRESERVATION OF NATURAL DIVERSITY THROUGH LAND PROTECTION

PHILLIP M. HOOSE
Island Press, Covelo, California

Printed in the United States of America

Library of Congress Cataloging in Publication Data

Hoose, Phillip M.   1947-
    Building an ark.

    Bibliography: p.
    Includes index.
        1. Nature conservation.   2. Landscape protection.
3. Natural areas.   4. Nature Conservancy (U.S.)
5. Nature conservation—Law and legislation.
I. Title.
QH75.H66   333.95'0973   80-28279
ISBN 0-933280-09-2

DEDICATION

To Robert C. Stover

TABLE OF CONTENTS

ACKNOWLEDGMENTS

The only real advantages I've had in writing this book are an adequate and secure source of funding for the project, skilled and caring editors, the best resource information available anywhere, a job that gives me the chance to travel widely and provides a daily working relationship with those who know most about the subjects I've described, and the support of a fine clerical staff. Otherwise, I did it all on my own.

I am most grateful for the constant encouragement and support of the Island Foundation, and particularly for the personal interest of Walter Sedgwick, who has a special feeling for the importance of expanding our ability to protect significant areas. Likewise, Barbara Dean and her colleagues at Island Press have demonstrated an intuitive feeling for the content of this book.

Among my colleagues at The Nature Conservancy I owe special thanks to Hardy Wieting, Jr., for schooling me in several concepts discussed in this book; to Greg Low, Loring Schwarz, Bill Burley, Dave Morine, John White, and Dennis Wolkoff for commenting extensively on chapter drafts; to Tom Massengale, John Humke, and Mike Green for providing case studies; to John Jensen for a detailed review of the chapter on lobbying; to Mike Dennis, the Conservancy's general counsel, who steered me through the acquisition chapter, frequently reciting from his frayed and yellowed copy of the tax code in hand (though he never seemed to be looking at it); to John Nutter for many insights; and to Lyn Lilly, who skillfully coordinated the physical production of a volume which passed through several drafts.

Jerry Paulson and Lydia Sargent Meyer of the Illinois Landowner Contact Program; Harry R. Tyler of the Maine Critical Areas Program; Charles E. Roe of the North Carolina Natural Heritage Program; and Rick Fortenberry, an attorney now practicing in Meridian, Mississippi, provided excellent drafts and materials on which portions of chapters were based. Ross Netherton and Professor Harold C. Jordahl, Jr., were instrumental in helping me organize the easement chapter. David Shupe of the Tennessee Heritage Program diligently helped me assemble a fact pattern contained in the case study in Chapter Thirteen. Robert Satter, for 16 years associated with the Connecticut legislature, offered an insightful review of Chapter Twelve.

ACKNOWLEDGMENTS

I owe special thanks to two individuals. Robert E. Jenkins, Vice-President for Science for The Nature Conservancy, has deepened continually my appreciation of the three premises that underlie this book: namely, that the preservation of ecological diversity is tremendously important; that the status of diversity on the natural landscape can be discerned at a given time; and that there are many incentives inherent in law, administrative policy, and human nature that can be used together as a system to protect the remainder of our ecological heritage. Much of this volume, particularly as it pertains to the linkage between ecological data and land conservation, is based on his insight. The second individual is my wife, Shoshana. Herself a writer, she read more drafts than anyone, helped me streamline the manuscript, and turned months which could have been merely bearable into a very enjoyable time for me.

Phillip M. Hoose
April 24, 1980
Arlington, Virginia

INTRODUCTION

This introduction is being written on April 23, 1980, one day after the celebration of the tenth anniversary of "Earth Day." The newspapers and public radio stations are full of tributes to the seventies as an environmental decade, citing as evidence of progress and elevated public sensitivity a series of laws that passed during the seventies, regulating mainly the speed with which humans can do themselves in.

During that same decade, there was progress on another front, namely, the ability to identify and protect what remains of America's natural ecological diversity. Though the radio is silent on this issue, the progress was important, since it is among the species of plants and animals, and the communities and ecosystems in which they function, that we usually find medicines, crops, and the agents that can resist blight and infestation of crops.

For the most part this progress has been accomplished without conflict and has in fact depended upon a characteristically pleasant relationship between public agencies and private citizens. Since most plants, animals, and ecosystems native to the United States can best be protected by conserving the specific areas of land that provide their biological requirements, and since all land in the United States is owned by someone, logic has drawn conservationists to the real estate market, a workplace Americans seem to enjoy.

During the environmental decade, conservationists tried to acquire thousands of property tracts. The most creative conservationists were usually able to acquire property at far less than market value by being able to help landowners take full advantage of the tax laws that encourage donations of land. In fact, some negotiators learned the Internal Revenue Code almost by rote. Their ability was further expanded by an Internal Revenue Service ruling, which clearly allowed deductions for donations of conservation easements, and by the advent of the Land and Water Conservation Fund, which toward the end of the decade provided a stable source of acquisition money.

Concurrently, we increased our ability to determine which places are most important to protect. In 1976 The Nature Conservancy piloted in South Carolina a system of gathering and managing information on natural ecological diversity within a state, and called the concept a "State Natural Heritage Program."

The program was established to help the state locate and monitor its ecological heritage and also to guide conservationists in choosing where to spend time, effort, and money. Heritage programs have now been replicated in 23 other states and by the Tennessee Valley Authority. Because the data are managed identically in all states, heritage programs have provided a good start toward a national inventory of ecological diversity.

A more sophisticated knowledge of the status of natural diversity has made life easier for negotiators in one sense and probably more difficult in another. On one hand, specific information about the relative significance of a population or community occurring on a property gives a conservationist a calling card, in that the ability to state that someone's bog is one of three places in the whole state where a bog community is known at least establishes a legitimacy of concern. At best such information shifts the discussion from "what are you doing here?" to "what can we do to protect something so special?"

On the other hand, conservationists find it challenging to protect within ecological boundaries oddly shaped fragments of tracts owned by people they have never met. For some owners, even the tax code provides no answers.

And so conservationists have explored other incentives for property owners. They have found that some landowners unwilling to hand over a deed will respond to offers of recognition, information, management assistance, and/or property tax relief. Some agree to surrender control of particular interests in property. Others will rent property for long periods.

Accordingly, in the 1970s many states passed laws and established outreach programs designed to expand their ability to protect elements of natural diversity even as they were learning more about the status of diversity in their states. Private conservation groups and public agencies at all levels of government increased their ability and resolve to set aside significant areas through administrative rules.

Since 1970:

1. Three states have begun systematically to notify all owners of significant areas within their state.
2. Twelve states have passed statutes creating nature preserves systems.
3. At least ten states have begun programs designed to honor owners of significant natural areas who sign voluntary protection agreements.
4. More than 20 states have enacted conservation easement laws, al-

lowing at least some nonprofit organizations to hold easements in gross.

5. The National Natural Landmark Program, begun by the National Park Service and now administered by the Heritage Conservation and Recreation Service, has registered over 300 properties through voluntary agreements.

This book explores several approaches available to conservationists working to protect significant areas. It is written mainly for professionals, but it should also be useful and interesting to laypeople who would like to add dimension to their understanding of land conservation. The book presents a series of options that can be used to build a strong program for the preservation of a state's natural ecological diversity.

The "tools," as they are called throughout these pages, have been selected mainly for their versatility. Each has worked successfully somewhere within a program. Their success does not seem to depend upon application within a particular region of the country, although some tools will work better in some places than in others.

Each tool can be used separately as a negotiating option; and all can be used together as a system of incentives. Some of the approaches discussed do not involve money or interests in real estate at all. Instead, by honoring and recognizing owners of significant property tracts, they encourage the voluntary protection of natural elements. The voluntary incentives discussed most thoroughly in Chapter Six should be especially interesting to lay readers because they offer real opportunities for the involvement of nonprofessionals.

Each tool described varies in terms of the strength, duration, speed, and cost of protection. The few states which have begun to use them together as ways to protect areas identified through an inventory are the leaders in the field of ecological conservation.

The first chapter presents a rationale for the preservation of natural diversity. Chapters Two and Three consider heritage programs and how they can be used to identify areas of critical importance. Chapter Four discusses the need for expanded protection options; Chapters Five through Eleven explore specific tools; Chapter Twelve attempts to offer a crash course in lobbying. Chapter Thirteen considers the potential application of ecological data, and Chapter Fourteen offers a model for using all the tools together in a hypothetical state.

Each discussion of a conservation approach attempts to convey, through case studies and anecdotes whenever possible, a sense of what has gone right and wrong, what has been tried and what has not, how much it has cost, and the ideal circumstances for their use. It is hoped this book will have a pollinating effect, acquainting conservationists unable to travel widely and frequently with ideas attempted by colleagues in other states or regions. Ideally these chapters will promote discussion and experimentation. For example, it might be difficult but useful for someone beginning a registry program in West Virginia to know that considerable wisdom—the stuff by which mistakes are avoided—is available in Indiana, Maine, and North Carolina, wisdom gained through trial, error, and refinement. For this reason names and addresses of key contacts appear at the end of the book.

It might be useful to say what this book is not. It is not an encyclopedia of planning tools but is, instead, a discussion of a limited group of options, each having at least a brief track record and apparent versatility. Planners may lament the absence of a few old friends.

This book also is not a discussion of the biological issues associated with land conservation. These chapters rather arbitrarily accept the United States as their domain—even though there may be a greater diversity of species within a square mile of a tropical forest than in certain physiographic regions of the United States.

The book likewise does not discuss the particular problems of protecting aquatic species and habitats, wide-ranging species, migrating species, or, perhaps most important, the entire area of stewardship. Just because something has been protected by law or consent does not mean nature will cooperate forever, or that factors humanly induced but beyond our ability to control through land conservation—such as acid rain—will not have the final word. The design and management of viable nature preserves, established to protect specific species and communities, we hope will provide grist for many authors and thesis writers of the 1980s.

Finally, except for a chapter on how state natural heritage programs can be used to organize an environmental review effort, this book does not deal with environmental regulation or litigation. Many useful volumes have been written on these subjects.

Today, ten years after Earth Day, the radio brings voices that reminisce, a little wistfully it seems, about heads lowered and antlers locked in battle, dams defeated at the last moment, and regulations forged in the heat of litigation. Despite the exhilaration of battle and the achievements won, especially in the area of public health, some of the speakers characterize the seventies as "years of net slippage."

They may be right, but the seventies also brought a measure of progress that has gone unheralded. During the decade, as a result of considerable vision, cooperation, and imaginative funding arrangements, Americans became much better able to identify which components of our common ecological heritage are in greatest jeopardy and how we can effect a rescue.

Those most responsible for this progress realized that it is futile to flail upstream against all the momentum of development in order to preserve natural diversity. It is necessary only to breast the tide in places and make it wash around instead of over the spots containing the species and systems requiring protection.

By continuing to improve our vision of the landscape and applying our imagination as we did in the last decade, we can probably hold on to what has been described as the last of the least and the best of the rest. The following chapters will present options for the preservation of natural diversity in the United States. We hope those who use them will provide hearty reminiscences for the columns and broadcasts of April 23, 1990.

CHAPTER ONE

THE PRESERVATION OF NATURAL DIVERSITY

Why Save Diversity?

What good is a snail darter? As practical men measure "good" probably none. But we simply don't know. What value would they have placed on the cowpox virus before Jenner; or on a penicillium mold (other than those inhabiting blue cheese) before Fleming; or in wild rubber trees before Goodyear learned to vulcanize their sap? Yet the life of almost every American is profoundly different because of these species.

James L. Buckley[1]

The reasons for saving natural diversity are in themselves diverse. The rationale, partly utilitarian and partly philosophical, includes at least the following considerations.

Human Nutrition Depends upon Diverse Genetic Resources

Only 20 species of plants now account for 90 percent of the world's diet. Small grains such as wheat, corn, and barley have become the mainstays of human subsistence. They are most productively grown in monocultures, but monocultures are easy prey for pests and diseases. Agricultural scientists can use progenitors of existing crops to breed disease-resistant strains, but as wild habitats vanish, this material is running out.

As recently as 1970, one-fifth of the United States' corn crop was eliminated by a corn blight. Only a change in the genetic makeup of the hybrid corn by breeding with wild progenitors allowed a stronger hybrid to develop.[2]

Pests and diseases are every bit as sophisticated as plant breeders, and the two groups have become engaged in a genetic chess match; scientists seem to be able to breed defenses only slightly faster than pests and diseases can decipher their codes. Only by protecting a broad range of plant material can we preserve the genetic stock upon which human survival ultimately depends.

Plants and Animals Provide Most of Our Medicines

Each species is a potential source of human medicine. Many medicines have come from very unlikely sources. Some examples involving animals include the following:

1. The armadillo is used in leprosy research because it has a high tolerance to that disease.
2. Blood of the horseshoe crab is used to diagnose spinal meningitis in children.
3. A substance that holds barnacles on rocks is being studied as a dental adhesive.
4. The electric organs of the electric eel are used in the treatment of muscle disease.
5. The nearly extinct desert pupfish may prove beneficial to human kidney disease research because it can tolerate extremes in temperature and salinity.
6. Bee venom is used to treat arthritis.
7. Blowfly larvae secrete the substance alantoin, which promotes the healing of deep wounds.

Plants are just as important. Prescriptions obtained from higher plants alone have an estimated market value of $3 billion. Of 76 major pharmaceutical components obtained from higher plants, only seven can be synthesized at competitive prices. Organic alkaloid compounds, found in almost 20 percent of all plant species, are used as painkillers, antimalarials, cardiac stimulants, blood pressure boosters, pupil dilators, muscle relaxants, local anesthetics, tumor inhibitors, and antileukemic drugs. So far only 2 percent of the earth's plants have been screened for alkaloids.[3]

Plants and Animals Serve Humankind and Offer Clues for Human Survival

We don't always notice the many ways that plants and animals serve us, nor do we often glimpse the full potential of any species for human benefit. It is safe to say that most denture wearers chat and dine all day without a passing thought for those barnacles who martyred themselves to provide adhesive. It is much easier to calculate the putative benefits of a dam or a highway than to appreciate the full value of the habitat to be lost. Furthermore, we cannot always know the role of a species within a total ecosystem. Plants and animals cannot tell us what they mean to each other.

Each species that has managed to persevere through the ages to share the earth with us now is a success story. We need success stories. Each of our cohabitants has evolved an ingenious and revealing set of life strategies.

If we look hard enough, each survivor can tell us something, often something we need to know. Some lichens wither if exposed to low concentrations of nitrous oxide. Some cave dwellers can help to indicate groundwater pollution. Cells of hairs on the pollen-bearing stamens of the spiderwort, a common roadside plant, mutate from blue to pink when exposed to even minute quantities of ionizing radiation. Honey can be used to monitor heavy metal pollution.

We can best preserve and study species by preserving the natural ecosystems to which they belong. Like species, natural systems have been working essentially in their present forms for millions of years; and they, too, offer clues to the traits that might ensure human survival. Ecosystems are highly evolved associations of species and inorganic landscape components uniquely adapted to specific parts of the earth's surface. They undoubtedly possess species and properties of which we are totally ignorant. Mankind simply cannot accurately duplicate natural ecosystems artificially. We must study species primarily in their natural environments if we are to gain all available knowledge from them.

Species and Natural Systems Have Intrinsic Value

The statements above have considered what plants and animals can do for us. Beyond this, species and systems should be allowed to persist simply because they exist now. We feel twinges of guilt about the plight of large creatures, usually snarling and irascible predators that are the first animals children come to know and which later become the mascot names of their schools. Why should we feel differently for small creatures, less sensational, overlooked, but here with us nonetheless?

All living things possess an intrinsic value which is beyond calculation. Humans as rational beings are responsible for safeguarding forms of life which we did not create but suddenly have the power to destroy. By knowingly causing the extinction of these species and their habitats, we sacrifice a part of our humanity.

Natural Diversity Is Urgently Threatened

In settling the continent, our pioneer ancestors tilled any field that a plowshare could withstand and cut nearly every tree within reach. One Ohio account conveys the passion of settlement.

3

Another innovation was used in northern Ohio where the land was nearly level. Selected trees were notched for felling, but not deeply enough for them to fall in calm weather. Leaving the forest for squall winds to complete the work, the settlers kept out of the woods during severe storms. Eventually there would be the crashing of tree crowns, monarchs of the forest falling like close columns of dominoes on edge, one against the other. Smaller trees were jumbled like jack-straws in a heap. When dry enough, the whole deadening would be set ablaze in one immense fire.[4]

No match for such intensity, the great virgin forest that once covered North America now survives in deep ravines or atop slopes too steep to provide secure footing. The remnants of the great tallgrass prairie that once covered much of the Midwest are now detected in subacre ceme-teries and in scattered strips along railroad rights-of-way.

Fur-bearing creatures haven't fared much better. Henry Fairfield Os-born and Harold Elmer Anthony observed in 1922 that:

Nothing in the history of creation has paralleled the ravages of the fur and hide trade, which, with the bone fertilizer trade, now threat-ens the entire vertebrate kingdom.[5]

Mr. Anthony set out to measure the extent of the slaughter. By tallying figures published in the *Fur Trade Review*, the leading fur industry peri-odical of the time, he calculated that over 107 million skins were sold be-tween 1919 and 1921, almost exactly one fur for every American citizen of 1920.[6]

If anything, contemporary Americans have picked up the pace. Hu-man enterprise has devastated several natural systems. Many southeastern streams have been straightened into muddy trenches with soy fields planted right up to their banks. The ground water of New Mexico's northwestern quadrant is being pumped so furiously that some observers fear the total depletion of the aquifer by the year 2000. Much of this water is being pumped out of the mines and left to evaporate in nearby arroyos so that miners can get to uranium ore. Already aquatic habitats are drying up, and waterside species are giving way to plants and animals that can take root in dryer conditions.

Brisk markets for softwood paneling and plywood have prompted tim-ber companies in the southeastern United States to plant and cut every 30 or so years vast fields of loblolly and slash pine trees in areas where mixed hardwood stands grow naturally. More than one wistful observer calls these solemn regiments of adolescent pine "dress-right-dress forests."

And as natural habitats have shrunken and become contaminated, many species have been reduced to submarginal status. The present global rate of species extinction—about one species gone per day—is a thousand times faster than it was before human settlement. Large predators are all but gone in most parts of the world. Most of Hawaii's native bird population is lost forever.

Species that require special food or habitat are hit hardest. For instance, the ivory-billed woodpecker, addicted to a particular type of grub, which infests only freshly dead trees, is probably now missing from the last patches of the once vast Mississippi River bottomland hardwood forest.

Humans are altering—biologically or in terms of use—nearly every acre of the American landscape. Between 1967 and 1975 almost 14 percent of the nonfederal land in this country—about 210 million acres—was converted from one use to another, forest to cropland, cropland to timberland, fields to desert, fields to shopping centers.[7]

One official in charge of a system of nature preserves in Illinois reports that his staff now spends as much time defending the borders of the preserves against various encroachments as they did in establishing the preserves.[8] A 1978 survey reported that 55 of the 455 National Natural Landmarks established since 1963 by the National Park Service are threatened or have already been damaged by mining and other forms of development.[9]

Summary

In short, most of America's native ecosystems and many of their constituent species have been broken or buried in the stampede of civilization. The importance of these populations and systems to human welfare and, indeed, human survival has been all but ignored, and their intrinsic importance is not currently acknowledged.

CHAPTER TWO

STATE NATURAL HERITAGE INVENTORIES

Let us hereby establish as our goal the preservation of at least one viable population of every plant and animal species now present in the United States, as well as the preservation of an excellent representative example of each distinctive community of plants and each aquatic ecosystem now present in the United States. In a sense we are attempting to build a second ark, protecting America's biological resources against a steady rain, which has been falling for some time. Our job will be even more difficult than was Noah's. Our ark will be fashioned of laws, deeds, and agreements; and many of the things we will usher aboard will be hard to locate or even recognize. We must plan carefully to construct our vessel; it is bound to be oddly shaped. Before applying hammer to nail, we will require:

1. An inventory of the species, communities, and natural systems of the United States, telling us where to look for the natural elements we wish to protect, and which examples of each are the best.
2. A process of analysis that we can apply to this inventory, so that we can board first the creatures most immediately in need of help. The starling is indeed a bird species, but it seems to be managing all right on its own for now. Even Noah didn't usher fish aboard his ark.

Working State by State

Our effort is best organized state by state since the resources required to inventory and protect natural elements are best organized and most available at the state level. Most biological data have been collected within a particular state, either within a state university system or within institutions such as state herbaria or natural history museums.

The scientists needed to identify critical natural elements and to establish and adjust the boundaries of protected sites frequently work for state institutions. Many individuals and charitable institutions will support projects only within a particular state. In many states laws have established agencies that are authorized to protect a state's natural resources.

Zoning and land use powers are usually concentrated within state jurisdictions. State pride is important too. Many people whose help we will need seem to think of themselves first as the resident of a state—as Hoosiers or Ohioans rather than midwesterners.

An Inventory of Natural Diversity

How do we know what is most important to protect in a given state? We will have to make choices, especially when it comes time to spend money to acquire property. Which natural elements should we protect first? Birds? Plants? Swamps? Forests? Which forests?

The scientists we consult are all convincing, but they don't seem to agree with one another. Ornithologists drag us through marshes at dawn. We crawl anxiously behind herpetologists into small openings in the ground. Botanists lead us warily to favorite research areas. Forest ecologists stand proudly beneath giant trees. But it is difficult to evaluate and compare unlike entities—trees to snakes, oxbows to nesting areas. No individual seems to have the perspective to organize our plan. We need a process that reduces natural phenomena to a common denominator so we can compare them.

State Natural Heritage Programs

As of March 1980, 23 states and the Tennessee Valley Authority had adopted a system pioneered by The Nature Conservancy for gathering, storing, and managing information on natural ecological diversity; it is called a "State Natural Heritage Program." Because the strategies described in the following chapters are based upon the availability of information organized in a heritage format, the program bears explanation.

Heritage programs manage information on "elements of natural diversity," which include rare animal species, rare plant species, the various types of native plant communities that remain within a state (such as certain prairie associations surviving in the plains states), and aquatic systems (such as interdunal pools or freshwater marshes).

A plant or animal species qualifies as an "element" only after committees of scientists have reviewed the fauna and flora of their state to produce a list of the declining, rare, and/or endangered species whose condition should be monitored. Thus, again, the starling is not apt to become an "element" in a given state because it is unlikely that ornithologists will perceive a need to manage data on starlings.

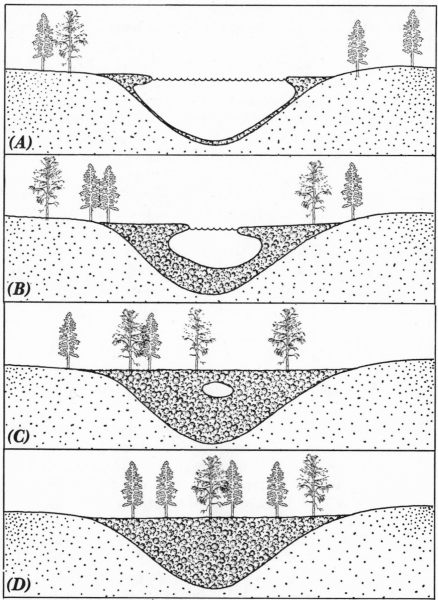

A bog lake succession. A floating mat of vegetation advances out over the water surface in a small lake in a cool, humid climate [A]. As the mat advances farther and the lake ages [B] and [C], scarcely decomposed organic matter (peat) accumulates in the lake basin, until after some thousands of years, the lake will be converted to forest [D]. Reprinted with permission of MacMillan Co. Inc., from *Communities and Ecosystems*, second edition, by Robert H. Whittaker. Copyright © 1975 by Robert H. Whittaker.

All plant community types represented within a state's overall vegetation and all aquatic systems present in a given state become elements as well, present within the data base as types. Thus, it is possible to collect data on excellent stands of the beech-maple forest type in Indiana, just as it is possible to document locations of rare orchids or mollusks.

It might seem illogical to collect data both on communities and species since communities can be viewed as dynamic associations composed of fairly constant species; but in the highly disturbed conditions that characterize most of the American landscape, ecosystems are frequently incomplete, and species turn up in surprising places. If we could protect viable occurrences of each plant community represented in the state, we would have fashioned a "coarse filter," capturing most but not all of the species.

Heritage programs thus allow the comparison of like entities—the elements of natural diversity—in terms of their rarity, relative endangerment, the factors which threaten them, and their biological vulnerability. Since nearly half the states have heritage programs now, exchange of regional information on elements is common practice.

An Inventory of Occurrences

A comprehensive effort to protect the best examples of the elements of a state's natural diversity begins logically with an inventory of the occurrences of each element. To plan wisely we must know where each element occurs within the state and be able to compare the merits of one place against another, just as we have developed a basis for comparing the importance of protecting one element against another.

In organizing a protection effort in Florida it would be important not only to be able to state, for example, that right now it is more urgent to try to protect the Everglades kite than the American alligator, but also to determine which of the areas or combination of areas in Florida known to be critical to the survival of the kite offers the best chance to protect a viable population.

The specific place where an element is reliably and repeatedly found is called an "element occurrence." (The sight of a bird winging overhead is not an occurrence, but a regularly used nest would be, if the species were considered important enough for special attention in a given state.)

Heritage workers record on a complete set of United States Geological Survey 7½-minute quadrangle maps all the element occurrence informa-

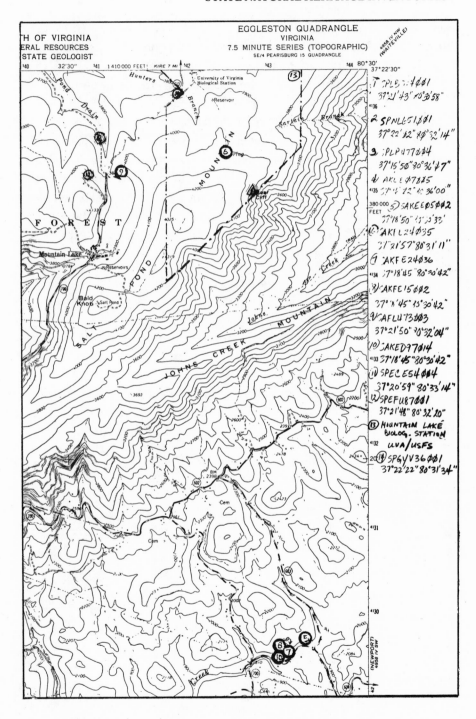

EGGLESTON QUADRANGLE
VIRGINIA
7.5 MINUTE SERIES (TOPOGRAPHIC)
SE/4 PEARISBURG 15 QUADRANGLE

11

tion available from primary (recent fieldwork) and secondary (scientific literature, herbaria, interviews with scientists, conference proceedings) sources. The quality and quantity of the information increase as the heritage data base matures. Each field season provides an opportunity to verify dubious or old occurrence records, to look for new occurrences in promising places, and to scour the undersurveyed areas in the state.

Information is gathered on elements which occur on both privately and publicly owned land, and without regard to how the land is managed. If it is certain that an area is being managed deliberately to protect an element occurrence, that fact is noted on the data collection sheets describing the occurrence. Such knowledge is essential. A grassland type represented on seven different nature preserves within a state probably does not require further attention right now.

Summary

In short, heritage data allow us to monitor the status of the natural diversity of a given state. Both the landscape and the status of our knowledge change continually, and heritage inventories are able to reflect these changes. They are not always changes for the worse. In Ohio 28 plants assumed to have been extirpated from the state were rediscovered between 1977 and 1979. We need to know when populations are destroyed, threatened, protected, or newly discovered, as well as which portions of the state have been so poorly studied that intensive field work is needed.

CHAPTER THREE

ORGANIZING A STATEWIDE PROTECTION PROGRAM

Assuming that each state should build an ark of its own, the heritage program office is a good place to begin construction. It is possible to start by searching the data to find what appear to be the best occurrences of each natural element and to determine whether each element is already protected adequately, as the fictitious example below will demonstrate.

Suppose the hypothetical Transylvania Heritage Program currently maintains mapped occurrence records for 500 elements of the state's natural diversity, including 280 plant species (about 10 percent of the state's flora), 100 animal species, 90 plant community types, and 30 aquatic systems (such as an oxbow lake).

The heritage staff is able to produce an "element status summary sheet" concisely displaying available information on the recorded occurrences of each of the 500 natural elements. Table 1 is a reproduction of an element status summary sheet for one prominent Transylvanian animal species, *Desmodus rotundus*, the vampire bat.

Desmodus rotundus has at least one viable population—at the Dismal Swamp Nature Preserve—protected as a natural area. Looking similarly at status summaries for each of Transylvania's 500 elements, we find that 102 of them occur in at least one place that can be considered "protected." We have not assumed that any population is protected merely because it occurs on public land. (A bird that happens to nest in a forest service unit scheduled for cutting had best be looking for a new home.) We have not considered any element occurrence to be protected unless we know that its habitat is managed deliberately for its perpetual protection.

We can next turn to the remaining 398 Transylvanian elements for which there is no record of a protected occurrence. In so doing we discover that some places contain healthy populations of more than one of those elements. Indeed our analysis of the heritage data shows that if we could establish preserves at 180 places, we could protect good occurrences of the 398 unprotected elements. But some of the data are too old to be absolutely reliable. To be certain that the species and communities have persisted in good condition, teams of field scientists penetrate the swamps and forests of Transylvania, squinting through miasma in search of plants and animals that were once reported to be at a spot, debating whether this or that stand remains the best example of a particular forest type, creating potential preserve boundaries, and finding out who owns the properties within them. To our disappointment they report that some occurrences are probably gone, but, hearteningly, they bring back some new records of fauna and flora that no one has seen for many years. Determined to include only sites that contain recently verified occurrences of underprotected elements, we trim our list to 125 sites. For the future the heritage program will continue to solicit fresh leads, and workers will try again next spring.

Using Heritage Data to Select Protection Priorities

When attempting to determine which sites are most important, that is, where to begin a protection program, the challenge becomes more complex, and analytical processes become more important.

A heritage data base should be regarded as a tool that can be used to simplify a difficult task, rather than as a magic box which can issue automatically a correct sequence of protection priorities. The data should focus, rather than substitute for, informed discussion. The following process of analysis, applied to a mature heritage program data base, should suggest protection priorities.

Selecting Target Elements. In deciding which elements—species, communities, and ecosystems—are most important to protect within a state, we can ask the following specific questions:

Which elements are rarest? For which elements have the fewest occurrences been reported? This factor considered alone can be misleading, particularly in dealing with a program that has not yet accumulated a great deal of data. Few occurrence records may in truth indicate that a certain portion of the state has not been adequately surveyed, or that little is known about a particular species, community type, or system.

What is the overall range of the element? The little bluestem prairie might occur in only one small lot in Indiana, but it may also have many larger examples just across the Illinois border. From the standpoint of distribution an element is of greatest interest if it is "endemic," or restricted to a state. Of somewhat less interest is an element in a state having popu-

16

Table 1

Species *Desmodus rotundus* SA41 .007
Element name and code

No.	Quad Name / Quad Code / County	Survey E or I	Info Date	Owner	Ensemble	Site Name / Site Status & Defensibility	Viability Quality & Defensibility	No. Occur in State (6)	No. Preserved Occurrences (1)	Source of Lead / Comments	Trans. Biol. Surv. Endangered / Element Status	Evaluation Recommendation	Preservation Priority
001	Last Ditch 398138 Pallor Co.	E	6/13/72	Jonathan Harker	*Solanum dulcamara* / *Amanita verna*	Several sightings near private home in disturbed area				Observed by Dr. Wolff Fangmier		Attempt to notify owner	
002	Melancholla 388266 Miasma Co.	I	6/27/77	International Paper Company	*Toxicodendron radicans* / *Toxicodendron vernix* / *Urtica dioica*	Extensive breeding population in large limestone caves				Dr. Horst Spelunk, Transylvania A & M		Excellent site IP has been notified	
003	Castle Run 388362 Doom Co.	E	6/24/74	Count Alacard	*Canis lupis var. homidae* / *Rattus norvegicus* / *Otus asio*	Many historical records near large castle. Field work apparently hazardous. Large dogs in area. Field accounts sketchy				Dr. Bram Stoker Gothic State Presbyterian College		Maintain status quo; well-established population	
004	Dismal Swamp 398216 Lucifer Co.		8/12/78	Transylvania Division of Nature Preserves		Dismal Swamp State Nature Preserve / Large, healthy population				Field surveyed by Dr. Wolff Fangmier, TSU in 1978		Monitor populations	
005	Phosphorescence 388285 Casket Co.		7/25/44	U.S. Forest Service	*Smilax hispida* / *Ulex europalis* / *Otus asio*					TSU Mammal Collection No. 47693, observable only in daytime		Reverify old record	
006	Neck Hair 398223 Cuspid Co.		7/7/56		*Canis lupis var. homidae*					Dr. Boris Stalactite Transylvania Teacher's College		Reverify old record	

lations that are "disjunct," or separated from the main body of its range. The greater the disjunction, the more significant the occurrences are apt to be because the disjunct populations, in adapting to their local conditions, are probably evolving genetic traits somewhat different from those common in the heart of the range. Also of less interest are elements in a state having "peripheral" populations on the edge of their range, such as the bluestem prairie cited above. Still, because genetic change tends to occur most rapidly at the edges of populations, peripheral occurrences can be important.

Is the element adequately protected in a given state or within its total range? It may be that even an element which is rare and endemic to a state has several viable examples protected firmly by law. In such an instance we may wish to move on to elements having more pressing problems. Again considering the total distribution of the element, we may decide that an element well protected within its total range—though not in our state—does not warrant immediate attention.

What is the official status of endangerment of each element? Each heritage program stratifies its lists of plant and animal species according to the degree of their endangerment. This stratification can help us arrange priorities. For example, we might look hard at species which have received national attention either through the Federal Endangered Species List or the Smithsonian List of Endangered and Threatened Plants. Some states also have lists of endangered plants and animals which receive some form of legal protection (see Table 1, Chapter Thirteen). Plant communities and aquatic systems are generally not assigned an official endangerment status.

Can the element be protected by any action we can take? Year after year the Ohio heritage program selects Big Darby Creek as a priority for protection because a stretch of it contains several federally endangered mollusks, which are known to occur only at that spot. Still, Ohio conservationists have long been at a loss to figure out how to protect these animals. At the site Big Darby is hardly a creek but is instead a wide and muddy stream flowing just east of the city of Columbus. It is polluted and frequently proposed for impoundments. The case illustrates that the problems afflicting some elements—particularly aquatics—are difficult to solve through land conservation. Protecting these aquatic elements may be the greatest challenge conservationists will face in the near future.

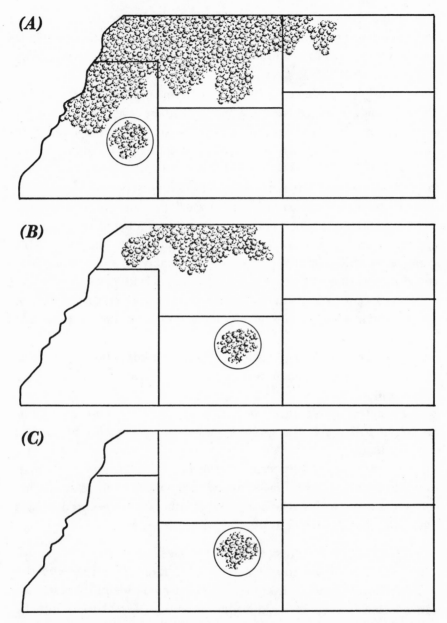

Distribution of a particular population from the perspective of five states. In Figure A, the circled population is peripheral to populations within the major extent of its range. In Figure B, the circled population is disjuncted from populations within the major extent of its range. In Figure C, the circled population is endemic to the state at lower center (assuming the species occurs nowhere else).

Selecting Target Occurrences of the Priority Elements. The process outlined above should have narrowed the field to elements in immediate need of protection. To determine which occurrences are most promising, we can ask the following questions:

How recently was the occurrence reported? Some reports will be too old to use as a basis for immediate decisions. If there are several recent records of occurrences, we might set the old records aside and arrange to return to the site in order to verify their continued existence. Caution: Just because a record is old does not mean it is invalid. In the summer of 1979, the Indiana heritage program rediscovered plants reported from 1837.

Are the occurrences known to be viable at all sites reported? Can they reproduce? An area may be so heavily disturbed, or a population so small, that reproduction is impossible at a site. The data may or may not be able to provide detailed information about the quality of a population at a site. However, there will be recorded information leading you to the individuals best acquainted with the site and with the species, community, or system. And it is likely that some of them will be in the room during your discussion.

Can the occurrences be defended at all sites reported? A threat may be so persistent, severe, or ominous at one place that there is no choice but to move on to another.

Which occurrences represent the best examples of a community type or the largest population of a species? This is simply a quality factor. We want the best.

Are there other significant occurrences nearby? Heritage programs map all occurrence data, and thus it is easy to see whether there are occurrences of other elements at or near the site. Other factors being equal, it is logical to protect as much as possible with one action.

Factors in Preserve Design

The questions above should have isolated target occurrences of the most significant elements. Even though we have now identified places toward which we can direct our immediate attention, we still need additional information before we can start to protect them, namely:

1. The ecological boundaries for a preserve at each site.
2. Knowledge of who owns the property tracts within each set of boundaries.

3. A sequence of tract protection. Are there any properties that, for ecological reasons, are more important than the others?

You will notice that in asking all of these questions we have tightened our focus increasingly, looking first at elements, then homing into specific occurrences, and now we are about to lock down onto property tracts. But before meeting or even identifying landowners, let's ask a few more questions as we draw ecological boundaries.

What is our objective at this site? What do we hope to accomplish in attempting a protection effort at a particular site? The primary objective should be the protection of an occurrence of a specific element.

What do the element or elements require to live at this site? We must understand the reproductive biology of any target species and the dynamics of a plant community or aquatic system.

Can the target element remain viable without conscious and continual intervention? Is the target element of a transitory sort? In 50 years will it have been destroyed by natural processes without management intervention? Are we able to do what will need to be done?

What is the minimal amount of land required to support the target element?

Beyond the minimum, how large a buffer can we reasonably add to protect the core against encroachment? The word "reasonably" is used because it never seems that one can offer enough security. Entire watersheds and subsurface drainage patterns usually dictate the ultimate health of an occurrence, but it is hard to control that much land.

Having drawn ecological boundaries, we can now find out who owns the property within them and begin to formulate strategies for building nature preserves. This entire process is modeled in Chapter Fourteen, along with the calculation of how much it would cost to protect natural diversity in a given state by adopting different protection strategies. In the following chapters we will consider a broad range of protection strategies.

Summary

A reasoned analysis of heritage program data can identify the elements in most immediate need of attention and can identify places where those elements can best be protected. Having a clear objective in mind, we can then visit the places identified and design ecological boundaries required to protect and buffer the targeted occurrences. It then remains to determine who owns the property tracts within the boundaries and to consider which tracts are most important to the potential preserve before approaching landowners.

CHAPTER FOUR

WHY WE NEED MORE WAYS TO PROTECT LAND

A project in an Atlantic Coast state illustrates the potential complexity of protecting elements occurring on property having several owners. In 1977 the state's heritage program staff analyzed its data, identifying as of immediate importance a pond set deep within a series of sandy hills. The pond, long esteemed by regional ecologists, featured an excellent stand of Atlantic white cedar, disjuncted widely from its nearest relative. Robust populations of carnivorous plants had colonized the pond's fringes, but most important were clusters of an extremely rare plant, a relative of the wild blueberry, known to occur only within the pond's drainage.

A plant ecologist and a hydrologist worked quickly together to determine the critical ecological boundaries of an adequate preserve. They were most interested in maintaining "seepage slopes," or a constant condition of wetness on the ground, from the outermost extension of the cedar stand down into the pond itself. This constant condition of moisture seemed essential to the survival of both the cedar community and the rare plants.

The workers then sought stubbornly to unravel the thread of tract ownership within the boundaries. After several hours of effort, they identified nine separate owners within an area of about 200 acres. Subsequent contact enabled them to characterize these owners as follows:

Owner 1: A church. When contacted, trustees first expressed little interest in protecting the pond but later said they might cooperate if other owners were interested.

Owner 2: A bank trust. The trustee would not disclose the identity of the actual owner.

Owner 3: A sand and gravel company.

Owner 4, 5, 6: A woman in her 80s, her 89-year-old brother, and her daughter. They do not speak to each other and each suspects (perhaps rightly) the others of treachery.

Owner 7: He owns an auto body shop and a salty disdain for biological conservation.

25

Owner 8: A woman in her 50s who seems to have some interest in protecting the pond.

Owner 9: A couple, owners of a lumber company. Although they might be interested in protecting the undeveloped portion of their property, their will dictates that it cannot be divided.

The elements occurring at this site still have not been completely protected, and the progress so far has required imagination and persistence.

A Tradition of Conservation by Land Acquisition

Historically, most land that has been set aside in the United States for public use has been acquired "in fee" (that is, all rights in property have been transferred to the recipient). The federal government alone has acquired by purchase, gift, condemnation, or exchange about 57 million acres for use by various agencies (not counting any lands in the public domain).[1]

State and local agencies similarly have purchased about a million acres of private property per year since 1959 (far more than the federal government during the same period).[2] Likewise, private nonprofit organizations such as The Nature Conservancy have employed their tax-exempt status skillfully to acquire scenic and natural areas through various means.

So far, reliance on land acquisition has made good sense because funds have been available. Between 1965 and 1979, congressional appropriations for federal use of the Land and Water Conservation Fund (LWCF) —the fund used the U.S. Forest Service, the U.S. Fish and Wildlife Service, the National Park Service, and the Bureau of Land Management to acquire land for outdoor recreation—rose from $5.5 million to $360 million annually.[3]

LWCF money has also been available to states having an approved State Comprehensive Outdoor Plan. Between 1965 and 1979 over $2.5 billion was apportioned to states for acquisition, development, and planning projects. At this writing states are currently in the process of acquiring almost two million acres through nearly 7,000 projects.[4]

It has also made sense to acquire property because you can do what you want with land you own. Many real estate negotiators are skeptical of less-than-fee protection techniques, preferring to hold out for control of all rights to properties of interest. But there are some signs that inflated land costs, an uncertain level of future LWCF funding, growing project backlogs, and congressional rumblings inspired by public resistance to further land withdrawals are forcing decisionmakers to seek alternative ways to commit land to public purposes. Several major agencies now seem to be searching for alternatives to acquisition. Before examining alternative ways to protect ecologically important areas, let's examine more closely the factors that limit our ability to acquire property for conservation purposes.

Limits to Land Acquisition

Public Land Is off the Market. The federal government owns about 33 percent of all land in the United States, and the states own another 6 percent. Most of the land owned by public agencies is grazed, timbered, mined, farmed, or played upon. It is seldom managed to protect elements of natural diversity. Public land, except for a relatively few acres auctioned each year as surplus, is off the real estate market and thus cannot be acquired by conservation groups.

Many Owners Won't Sell or Donate Their Property. Natural elements have no notion of property. They array themselves according to their own logic. Rare grasses ripple through bombing ranges, and prairie fragments persist in old cemeteries; threatened songbirds breed along airport runways, and rare plants sprout ineffably in roadside ditches.

Not all private property in the United States is owned by families struggling to make mortgage payments. Five hundred sixty-eight giant companies control 23 percent of all private property. Over 94 million acres of government land have been given to railroads. To build our ark we'll have to understand and match the needs of corporate executives, tribal councils, forest supervisors, land speculators, heiresses, farmers, ranchers, and bureaucrats. Owners view their property in different ways, sometimes with a fierce emotional attachment. Some see property as a link to the past, others as a bridge to the future. Property owners want their land to be all sorts of things—a place to live, to work; a source of income now or someday; a source of continuity, food, security, investment income, serenity, beauty, or tax relief.

In short not all owners will want to hand over the deed, no matter how persuasive we are. We'll have to come up with some compelling alternatives for these owners. As one conservationist puts it, "You have to bait the hook to suit the fish." Clearly, we'll need a large tackle box.

We Don't Have Enough Money to Buy It All. Between 1967 and 1977 the total dollar value of land in the United States rose 154 percent —from $590 billion to $1.5 trillion. Between 1971 and 1975 assessed property values increased 45 percent. The average price of an acre of farmland in the United States rose 26.3 percent—from $388 to $490 (1979 figures).[5] In short, land is expensive, and it's not getting any cheaper.

There Is Increasing Opposition to Further Land Withdrawal. Of all land in the 13 westernmost states (including Alaska) 63.5 percent is federally owned. Most of this land, consisting mainly of pasturage, cropland, forests, parks, and refuges, is withdrawn from taxation and development.

The extent of public ownership of land in the West is a source of constant controversy. In 1979 the state of Nevada sued for possession of all federal lands within the state (86.5 percent of the land base). This action was the most conspicuous episode in what has been titled "the Sagebrush Rebellion."

Federal condemnation of property is especially provocative. In 1978 the justice department's Land and Natural Resources Division spent more than $58 million to acquire lands by condemnation for various federal agencies. These actions, taken generally as a last resort, drew more than 900 lawsuits. At the end of 1977 there were $500 million worth of claims alleging the government had taken private property without due compensation.[6]

There is also a tradition of resistance to the removal of property from the tax rolls by private groups. Churches and schools are usually singled out for scorn, but conservation groups own plenty of tax-exempt property and have themselves become popular targets.

Tax Laws Could Change. Nonprofit charitable organizations meeting standards described in section 501(c)(3) of the Internal Revenue Code consistently acquire land at a lower cost than it would bring on the open market because individuals and corporations who donate land to these organizations can write off the value of their gifts for federal income tax purposes, up to certain limits described in Chapters Nine and Ten of this book. Furthermore, the value of land donated to qualifying groups is sometimes exempted from property taxation.

Federal and many state tax laws generally encourage charity for public purposes, which include the preservation of lands for scenic, recreational, and scientific values. However, this may not be the case forever. Congress periodically reviews both the eligibility standards for 501(c)(3) groups and the incentives for donors, and restrictive changes could reduce the survival margin for nonprofit landholders. Likewise, sudden restrictive changes in state property tax laws could discourage charitable organizations with considerable holdings, thereby making it difficult for them to meet the tax bill.

Sometimes We Need to Act Quickly. When a species population or natural system is suddenly threatened, there may not be enough time to negotiate a gift or purchase of land. Generally, success is most likely when land and its owners are least pressured.

It usually takes a long time for public agencies to acquire land, whether at market value or below. Sometimes private lands in areas authorized for federal acquisition can be tied up for five to ten years before Congress gets around to appropriating the money. A three-year lag-time is common.

Four federal agencies—the National Park Service, the U.S. Forest Service, the U.S. Fish and Wildlife Service, and the Bureau of Land Management—together carried in the summer of 1979 a $2.2 billion backlog of projects authorized by Congress and scheduled for acquisition, presumably using funds to be provided by the LWCF. Even if no new acquisitions were authorized and the LWCF were to remain at present funding and land prices were to rise 10 percent annually, it would take until 1989 to acquire all this land.[7] Sometimes a qualifying nonprofit organization can help by acquiring and holding properties until public funds become available, but even the most solvent of private organizations cannot tap bottomless reservoirs of ready cash.

A System of Tools and Strategies

Given a limited ability to acquire property, we are obliged to develop techniques that vary in several fundamental ways.

1. The speed with which they can be used.
2. Their cost.
3. The strength of the protection they offer.
4. The duration of the protection they offer.
5. The degree to which they restrict a deed.

In addition, we need tools to protect elements occurring on public land.

Table 1 was derived from an effort conducted by The Nature Conservancy to protect a system of interdunal pools on the North Carolina coast.

29

It illustrates the importance of determining the needs and desires of each property owner within ecological boundaries and shows that it is possible to structure a protection option to address each individual situation. The techniques listed in the "approach" column are discussed in subsequent chapters.

Using the Tools Together

The next chapters describe a series of tools and derivative options—themes and variations. They can be used together as lures in our tackle box in any state, although patterns of land ownership will influence the relative proportion of their use. For instance, administrative designation of federal land, discussed in Chapter Seven, will mean more in Idaho (63.7 percent federally owned) than in Connecticut (0.3 percent federally owned).

The approaches to be described were chosen because they can be used in any state; they are not regionally selective. In the opinion of workers who have researched them and experimented with them, these tools are essential components of any comprehensive state natural area protection program. They offer landowners six kinds of incentives—information, recognition, cash, tax savings, property tax relief, and management assistance—to protect the natural elements occurring on their land. The tools can be used individually or in concert. Usually it will take time to build a preserve. Not every landowner will be bowled over by our introductory remarks.

This system of tools is designed to allow conservationists to secure from a landowner an early commitment to protection without having to negotiate for the deed to his property. These options can be used as blankets, cast one at a time over the years, protecting natural elements first by developing a solid relationship with those who own the property on which they exist.

Veteran real estate negotiators, their grizzled faces deeply lined, their memories long with deals made and just missed, might be inclined to mutter about these techniques, "This stuff is nothing new; we do this all the time," or "We've been using easements for years." They're right; each of the techniques described has some history of use, and it has been possible to find at least one case study for each tool.

They, too, however, would probably like to work within a program that allows them an expanded set of negotiating options. Too often, for example, state or federal agencies have launched an "easement program," sending negotiators into rural areas with instructions to bring back as many easement agreements as possible. Interviews with landowners usually have turned into discussions as to the local going rate for easements, with owners citing the lofty prices paid to their neighbors. Negotiators have had no fallback options in these instances.

Table 1

Landowner Needs and Matching Approaches

Parcel	Owner	Need/Desire	Approach
A	Elderly woman, no heirs	Top dollar	Purchase, although this land is bufferage and may not be essential.
B	Pennsylvania couple	Not yet fully known	Bargain sale, probably.
C	Husband and wife, the Smith family	Residence, land protection, some income	Obtain rights of first refusal until E is protected.
D	Two children and aunt, the Smith family	Some income, protection for natural features	Obtain rights of first refusal until E is protected, then bargain sale for conservation easement.
E	Owner of parcel A	Income	Purchase through bargain sale.
F	Wife, the Smith family, children will inherit	Kids want some income, rights of residency in a corner of property	Secure rights of first refusal, wait until J and E are protected, purchase conservation easement.
G	Uncooperative single man	Tax jam, needs quick cash, opposes conservation	Purchase through bargain sale.
H	A single woman	To build an alcoholic treatment center, but would avoid sensitive area	Tax-free exchange.
I	Wife, the Smith family	To build up to four structures on parcels C and D combined, to protect natural features	Secure rights of first refusal, wait until parcels J and E are protected, then obtain gift of conservation easement.
J	Two brothers	Have capital gains problem, need tax relief	Purchase at 50 percent bargain sale.
K	Single man, resident	Residence, is sympathetic to conservation	Negotiate nonbinding registration agreement.
L	Developer	To complete a subdivision already begun	Regulate through local zoning.

What is missing, then, is a comprehensive state protection program using a set of techniques within a *system*. Conservationists need to be able to weigh many options, one against another, in deciding how to initiate protection of a given area. They also need the ability to build a preserve over time, layering gradually the owner's commitment to conservation. The chapters ahead describe such a system, one tool at a time. The final chapter attempts to model how they can be used together dynamically to protect natural diversity in a hypothetical state.

Summary

The land on which rare species live and ecosystems function could be owned by anyone. To protect the natural ecological diversity of the United States we will need a set of tools that addresses the widely varying needs and desires of individuals, groups, corporations, and agencies. We are compelled to diversify our strategies beyond land acquisition because not all land is for sale, much of it is too expensive, withdrawal of private land is increasingly unpopular, tax laws are unpredictable, and sometimes there is not sufficient time to protect by acquiring property something immediately threatened. Within each state there is the need for a set of legal, administrative, and voluntary protection approaches that can function dynamically as a system.

CHAPTER FIVE

NOTIFICATION

More elements of natural diversity are destroyed through ignorance than through malice. Nearly everyone has heard horror stories about a habitat that was destroyed deliberately by landowners wishing to avoid property restrictions supposedly inflicted by the Endangered Species Act. We don't hear as much about the habitats that are destroyed every day by people who might well have adjusted their plans had they known that something special occurred on their property.

Notification refers to the act of informing a landowner that a natural element identified through an inventory process occurs on his property, telling him why it is important, and discovering his attitude toward this information. Notification can be distinguished from the other tools described in this book in that the landowner is not asked to *do* anything. He simply takes part in an exchange of information.

This initial exchange is crucial, both because a good first impression· can prevent the ignorant destruction of something very important and because it can establish personal relationships that might result eventually in stronger protection. Notification can thus be an end in itself or the foundation of a solid protection program.

The way in which landowners are notified is important to the success of a landowner contact program. The less bureaucratic the initial encounter, the better. A visit should be preceded by a brief, clear, and concise introductory letter (see Appendix A) sent by regular mail and by a phone call to secure an appointment. Most important of all is that the landowner meets the right person. A good listener in full command of the information he wishes to impart should be able to overcome the anxiety that is apt to well up in a landowner when a stranger appears to discuss his property.

The best contact person might be a peer or a friend, but it can be difficult to match each landowner with a peer who can describe a program effectively. Most landowner contact program directors have hired good communicators who can convey scientific information to all kinds of people in a respectful and disarming manner.

Timing is important. A landowner is most receptive when he and his property are least pressured. An owner who is about to sell his property to a developer is not as likely to be as interested in conservation as he would have been at an earlier hour. Furthermore, he might fear that his deal could collapse if word got around that his property contained something of biological significance.

A lot of preparation goes into an effective landowner contact program. The representative has to be credible. He must be able to tell the landowner why the swampy area by his woodlot is so important, and someone connected with the program—whether it is the initial contact or a scientist who appears at a later date—must be able to show him where the special elements are. Thus the information must be recent, accurate, mapped, and should be able to demonstrate the relative significance of any natural feature. It is a real advantage to be able to inform someone that his property contains one of the three known occurrences of a particular species or community type. A good inventory is the backbone of a successful notification program.

Information obtained in a first visit can be used to shape subsequent protection strategies. A good listener should be able to find out whether the owner is aware of the special elements and his attitude toward them, whether or not they have endured because the landowner has protected them deliberately, potential threats to the area, the landowner's needs and desires, and the pressures he experiences related to his property. Program representatives have discovered that many landowners are delighted to know that something special occurs on their land.

Case Study: The Illinois Landowner Contact Program

The Illinois Landowner Contact Program grew out of the Illinois Natural Areas Inventory, a three-year project conducted by the University of Illinois and the Natural Land Institute, jointly under a contract with the Illinois Department of Conservation. Researchers who sought to identify the best remaining natural areas in Illinois eventually identified 1,089 qualifying areas, the best 610 of which were called "Category I" sites.

About 300 Category I areas are privately owned. The field staff of the landowner contact program visited the owners of each of these areas to inform them that their lands are ecologically important and to determine their attitudes about preservation.

36

Startup Funding. A grant from a Chicago foundation provided about $150,000 to launch the program. The program director hired five field-workers in July of 1978. The state was divided into six regions, with each fieldworker assigned to contact the owners of private Category I areas within his region. One region was assigned to The Nature Conservancy, whose staff had worked with landowners in several northeastern Illinois counties.

The program's director had clear ideas about the qualities he desired in candidates for the field positions. First and foremost he sought people who could put other people at ease and who felt comfortable talking to many different types of people. He considered a background in biological sciences to be an important asset but not a requirement. Because the program's ultimate goal is to develop and implement a protection strategy for each area, the director sought bright, flexible people who could size up the landowner's financial situation and attitude toward conservation and who might eventually be able to negotiate protection proposals. Of the five people hired, two had backgrounds in psychology and three in biology.

Work Plan for the Program. The first workers were hired in July 1978. They spent July and August converting raw data from the Natural Areas Inventory into information packages for each privately owned Category I site. Each package contained a computer printout of site information, a copy of the site's topographic map, a completed field survey form, species lists, aerial photo, and overlays. The staff decided to conduct a pilot phase in 20 counties, with 3 or 4 counties in each of the six sections of the state. Eighty-one landowners were eventually contacted for 71 areas during the pilot phase.

Most of September and October were devoted to obtaining landowners' names and addresses from county courthouses. The staff tried to make sure that the landowner information was up-to-date and accurate. Copies of published plat book maps were used as the starting point for determining the landowner's name and address. The ownership was then checked against the records in the county assessor's office. If there was some question of ownership, a second check was made of deeds or probate records in the county recorder's office. It was also sometimes necessary to check the records of the county office of the Agricultural Stabilization and Conservation Service (ASCS) to verify the correct owner or boundaries of a given parcel of land.

It was important to avoid the impression that the staff members were land speculators or state agents. Usually the staff could find ownership information without assistance, but it was sometimes necessary to ask the courthouse staff to do the work. Other useful sources of landowner information were local telephone directories and the local post office. The county Soil Conservation Service district conservationist was also a good source of ownership information.

Ownership plat maps were drawn using the Illinois Natural Areas Inventory map as the base. Boundaries were drawn for each ownership parcel, and each parcel was given a number. An ownership data summary sheet was filled out for each parcel. Boundary information was obtained from tax maps, ASCS records, and published plat book maps.

Training for Contactors. The Natural Land Institute (NLI) conducted a two-day training workshop for the field staff. The workshop included a day on acquisition techniques (taught by a representative from The Nature Conservancy) but focused primarily on the psychology of dealing with landowners.

The director purchased (for about $150) a series of tapes and workbooks designed to enhance the worker's communicative skills. NLI believes that a worker who understands a landowner's emotional and psychological investment in his property — as well as his financial basis — will be better able to interest the landowner in protection.

According to the Landowner Contact Program director, the training seminar fell under the general rubric of "transactional analysis." There was considerable role playing. Above all, NLI was interested in knowing what a landowner needs.

Two fundamental decisions shaped the workshop's format. First, Illinois decided that the contactor should not ask the landowner to do anything during the first visit. The fieldworker was instead to provide information, to discover why the land had remained natural, to sense — without forcing the issue — the landowner's feeling about his land and his attitude toward protection, and to pave the way for a subsequent visit when a specific protection plan would be proposed.

Second, Illinois decided to rely solely upon paid staff members rather than volunteers to notify landowners. The NLI had the money to hire five fieldworkers and believed their staff could cover the whole state. The NLI did not attempt to develop a statewide network of volunteers to help the staff talk peer-to-peer with landowners. They instead sought to hire professionals who could be trained to cope with any situation.

The North Carolina Natural Landmark Registry Progam (NLRP) bears discussion here because it provides an interesting organizational contrast to the Illinois program. The NLRP, administered by the North Carolina Natural Heritage Program, was, like the Illinois Landowner Contact Program, established to interview hundreds of owners of properties identified as ecologically significant through a comprehensive statewide inventory. However, the NLRP takes the additional step of soliciting voluntary protection agreements from each owner (an idea that is the subject of the following chapter) and uses volunteers extensively.

The three members of the North Carolina Heritage Program staff realized from the beginning that, unlike the Illinois program, they could never mount an effective outreach solely through staff effort. They had no money to hire help, and felt a primary responsibility toward building and enriching the heritage data base. They decided to develop a statewide network of local volunteer experts to help verify the significance of promising areas and to introduce heritage staff members locally to landowners in order to "break the ice."

Through a series of seven regional workshops in North Carolina, and through the extensive scientific contacts the heritage program had developed, the heritage staff within a year or so was able to assemble nearly 60 professional scientists, amateur and professional naturalists, and conservationists from every corner of the state. (Interestingly, North Carolina has more university and college campuses than any state in the Union.) Many local consultants are professors and instructors. These individuals have contributed enormously to the early success of the program and have also helped devise management plans for some registered areas.

The decision as to which model or combination of the two to follow should probably depend upon the staff resources at hand, the money available in the state, and the organizational inclinations of the program director. It's nice, though, when possible, to have a broad base of support.

How Illinois Landowners Have Reacted to Strangers Coming to Call. The notification sequence begins in Illinois with a letter of introduction (see Appendix A). Some letters come back stamped "wrong address," but even this is instructive. About two weeks later a program representative follows with a phone call, opening with something such as, "I hope you got our letter; when I am in your area on October 14, I would like to stop by for a few minutes." Most landowners assent, but many others have said things such as, "Why do you have to come out here; can't you just tell me over the phone?" Moments like these test the representative's resourcefulness.

One fieldworker, Lydia Sargent Meyer, has kept a journal of her experiences with the landowner contact program. Of her first encounter with a landowner, she recalls:

> My first appointment was a three-hour drive from Rockford on a cold Tuesday in late November. I tend to relax while driving, but nevertheless I was very nervous (my journal for the night before says, "didn't sleep well"), and I stopped at a park to review my notes for the umpteenth time. I found the route to my appointment didn't look at all the way it had appeared on the county map and the way I had imagined it (assumptions at work!). The house was on a narrow, icy, gravel road perched on a Mississippi River bluff. After I had admired the gorgeous view, the owner, in his 80s, sat and listened. He finally said, "You ought to buy it; I don't want those city guys building out here. I'll sell it for a national park or whatever." I stayed half an hour and hoped I'd said the right things. He certainly had, but he looked as though he might not be around too long.

Lydia visited almost every person to whom she sent a letter. Another representative was denied an appointment only two or three times. In fact, fieldworkers generally succeeded in reaching the doorstep.

Sometimes fieldworkers found that they had inaccurate ownership information, and about 10 percent of the information found in published plat book maps at county courthouses contained errors. When faced with misinformation, workers turned to tax assessors, deeds, and probate records for more recent information.

Trying to find information on trusts and estates has been a problem. Usually the tax map shows the name of a bank instead of a person. This generally means that the owner has put his land into a trust, under the care of a bank. The bank pays taxes and handles other chores for a fee. Thus the NLI's initial letter goes to a bank, with a note asking the trust officer to pass the enclosed information on to the owner. It is then hoped that the owner will contact NLI. This, of course, seldom happens; it is far too impersonal. The owner has paid the bank to screen such letters. Letters to trust officers requesting disclosure of the owner's identity have drawn indignant replies.

One worker seeking such information has decided to visit trust officers personally, in hopes that the official will become interested in the land-owner contact project and will himself contact the owner. She takes care not to ask the banker to reveal the owner's identity. So far this approach has worked well.

Fieldworkers work about 40 to 45 hours a week. So far they have not had to work much at night or on weekends. Most owners have either ar-ranged to be home at an appointed time or allowed the worker to visit their workplace. In Illinois, the workplace has often been the farm. Farm-ers are most accessible in the winter, and are almost never available dur-ing planting or harvesting. The visits seem to average about 45 minutes.

After each visit the fieldworker writes a thank you note and drafts a trip report. The program director estimates that each contact, including the paperwork and the visit, takes about one working day. One worker said the figure is probably closer to a day and a half. Workers find it most effi-cient to spend two or three consecutive days in the field visiting landown-ers, then come back to the office for two or three days of paperwork.

So far women seem to have been more successful at contacting Illinois landowners than men. One fellow in particular has had serious problems converting phone calls into visits when women answer the phone. He hesi-tates to say, "May I speak with your husband?" because he fears that women (whom he will meet later) will resent the presumption that the man of the house speaks for their property. Some women have doubted his intentions when he has asked to visit.

The Illinois field representatives have by now developed an impressive body of experience, both scientific and anecdotal. Again from Lydia's journal:

> I have run into the whole gamut of awareness or ignorance of how special a landowner's property may be from an ecological point of view. Some people knew they owned something special; some didn't suspect that "that old weed lot" was anything significant. Most have been pleased to learn of the inventory's findings. One couple had bought 40 wooded acres along the Illinois River bluffs several years ago just for their own use. A hill prairie is on the property, and they were going to plant pine trees right in the prairie to fill up that weedy area. Now they are working with the county conservation district to restore the prairie.

Showing species lists to one landowner in particular helped hit home the fact that the land belongs to the person I'm contacting. You are visiting the owner to tell him about his or her land, and first and foremost you must respect the fact that he or she is the owner. No matter how badly you want to see an area preserved, it will not happen unless the owner shares that feeling. I feel the owner has the right to see the information we have about his land. I now determine how much data to show or give a contact, depending on my assessment of their interest and scientific sophistication. I think, though, that the more we share with them the more they realize the significance of the natural area and that a great deal of study went into the inventory. This also helps bolster our credibility. When interest is expressed in the plant species, I make a list of the common names of the plants for their area and send it to them with my thank you letter.

So far I have traveled 6,100 miles to visit landowners, visited with 72 private owners, 20 corporations, and done 14 phone interviews, half a dozen follow-up field trips, made innumerable phone calls, written innumerable memos and plant lists, and sent over a hundred personalized thank you letters. There have been other preservation activities, workshops, meetings. It has been a rich, exciting time for me.

Results to Date. After the first round of contacts had been completed in Illinois (it took about a year), the program staff produced the following tables as part of an effort to evaluate their experience and to plan subsequent action.

The Natural Land Institute, working with The Nature Conservancy, is now engaged in a second round of visits. This time a representative will propose a specific protection strategy to each landowner, based on the information obtained during the first meeting.

The Natural Land Institute, the Illinois Nature Preserves Commission and The Nature Conservancy work together in this effort. They are well equipped to succeed. The Illinois State Department of Conservation has a substantial acquisition budget and an impressive tradition of natural area activity. There is in Illinois a strong natural areas protection statute that establishes a system of nature preserves into which many areas have already been dedicated.

Illinois has not registered areas as of this writing, but the NLI is now preparing introductory materials and certificates of recognition for cooperating landowners. NLI will give cooperating owners a booklet contain-

Table 1
Illinois Landowner Contacts as of October 4, 1979

	No.	Percent
CONTACTS MADE	312	100
Ownership		
Individual	292	94
Corporation	13	4
Charitable group	7	2
Educational institution	0	0
Public corporation	0	0
Age Group		
20-39 years	18	6
40-59 years	110	35
60-80 + years	117	38
Unknown or did not answer	67	21
Length of Ownership		
Less than 10 years	55	18
10-39 years	68	22
40-69 years	50	16
70-100 + years	65	21
Unknown or did not answer	74	23
Reasons for Preservation		
Intentional	85	27
Difficult to exploit	164	53
Traditional	28	9
Land use pattern	12	4
Unknown or did not answer	23	7

ing a series of case studies describing the way landowners feel about having protected their land in various ways.

Setting Up a Landowner Contact Program

Suppose we wish to establish a statewide landowner contact program in a "typical" state (bearing in mind there is no such thing) beginning November 1. Here is how we might proceed.

Assumptions

1. There are 200 owners to contact, all of whom own property supporting the occurrence of an element of natural diversity.
2. We will contact both private landowners and managers of public lands containing element occurrences.
3. The expense of collecting, storing, managing, and analyzing data will not be charged against the project (this may not be a valid assumption in every state).

4. Scientific support will be available free of charge. Thus if we need a scientist to interpret a natural feature for a landowner, the expense (excluding travel and meals) will not be charged against the project.

Task 1: Selection of sites (by November 1).

It is probably best to begin about November 1 a landowner contact program that is focused around data provided by an inventory. Summer field investigations usually continue through September, and it takes at least a month to enter new data and compare it against existing records.

Task 2: Research of ownership (by January 1).

This involves numerous trips to county courthouses, banks, and planning offices. Good trip routing can reduce the duration of this task.

Task 3: Preparation of site reports (by February 1).

Someone has to combine ecological information provided by the inventory staff with maps and ownership data. How long this takes depends largely on how much information the inventory people have been able to provide. For each site there should be a package containing, at a minimum, (1) a brief statement of the significance of the site (a landowner has to know why his property is creating all the interest); (2) a map showing where the important features are located; and (3) the name and address of the owner, directions to the site, and anything else known about the owner (What does he do? When is he apt to be home?).

Caution: We should be sure that the occurrences are on the property before someone visits the owner. If in doubt, field check it over the summer and go back next year.

Task 4: Development of a file structure (by February 1).

There should be at least two kinds of files, tract files and tickle files. A tract file should contain at least (1) the site package described above; (2) an administrative history file kept at the front of the folder, listing on one sheet of paper the various steps included in the process of notification and the status of their completion; this sheet lets us know at a glance what remains to be done on any tract; and (3) a file for reporting what happened during transactions with landowners.

Tract files might best be arranged by county. Someone might forget an owner's name among 200, but he won't forget the county. Also, we might group the files for the tracts we're working on at a given moment in an "active" file drawer.

Table 2

Illinois Private Landowner Preservation Attitudes

COUNTY	Willing seller	Conservation easement	Potential donation	Interested in preservation	Not interested in preservation	Protected by owner	Threatened	Unknown
Cass	1					1	1	
Clark				1		2		
Coles	2	2	1	1				1
DeWitt			1					
Greene						1		
Grundy						1		
Hardin				2				
Henry			1	1				
Iroquois	1	1						
Jo Daviess	2							
Johnson	1		1	3			1	2
Kankakee	4	1	1					
Kendall						2		1
La Salle		1			1	1	1	
Lee			2	1		1		1
Livingston		1						
Macon		2	1					
Macoupin				3				1
Mason	2					7		2
Massac						3		
Menard				1				
Mercer				1				
Ogle	1	1		1		3		
Peoria	1	1			1	1		2
Perry		1		2			1	
Pope						2		
Pulaski					1			
Putnam	1		1	1		1		
Rock Island	3		1	1				
Stephenson		2						
Tazewell	3	1				1		
Union	1			1		1		1
Vermilion			1	1	1			
Washington				3				1
Will	1		1					2
Winnebago		1	1	3	1	2		
Woodford								3
Totals (135)	24	15	13	27	5	30	4	17
Percent of Total	18%	11%	10%	20%	4%	22%	3%	13%

"Tickle" files, arranged by month, are kept as a reminder that it is time to do something in particular. Suppose we plan to visit each landowner at least once a year. We need to know when each owner's year is up. This can be done conveniently by dropping an index card with the names of landowners contacted in November in the "November" file. Dentists are famous keepers of tickle files.

Good files are important. They are worth a lot of planning and attention.

Task 5: Production of project materials (by February 15).

A good program must have at least letterhead stationery and an attractive, brief, and readable brochure describing the program. These materials contribute to a solid, credible impression. They deserve time and thought.

Task 6: A trial run (letters out by March 1, follow-up phone calls by March 7, visits March 10 to 25).

We should start small and expand, beginning with a test spin on a reduced scale. Select 15 or so landowners that vary in representative ways, making the first few contacts easy just to work the bugs out. We might avoid notifying in the trial period the owners of the most significant natural features, just in case nervousness or inexperience overcome our representative.

Task 7: Regroup and evaluate (April Fool's Day).

Task 8: Full steam ahead (April 1 to May 31).

Plan efficient travel routes. Make a schedule and contact landowners in earnest. Devise a good reporting format for each contact, including categories for at least the following:

1. Owner's knowledge of natural feature.
2. Owner's attitude toward feature.
3. Owner's plans for property.
4. Short-term threats to natural features.
5. Long-term threats to natural features.
6. Property tax picture.
7. Estimated basis and value of property.
8. Comments.
9. Recommendations for stronger protection.

We might consider equipping a field representative with a dictaphone so that he can look at the format and dictate his comments immediately for subsequent transcription, either by the worker or a secretary.

Task 9: Follow-up (production of newsletter by May 31).

It is important to maintain contact with each owner. The best bets are

Table 3

Budget for a 1980 State Landowner Contact Program
(Duration: 18 months)

STAFF

1.	Project coordinator, 18 months @ $1,332/mo.	$23,976
2.	Field representative, 18 months @ $1,083/mo.	19,494
3.	Secretary, 18 months, 24 hours/wk. @ $500/mo.	9,000
	Benefits @ 18%	9,444
	Subtotal	$62,390

OFFICE

1.	Rent @ $2,000/yr. (assumes sharing of existing office space)	$ 3,000
2.	Typewriter $1,000/yr.	1,500
3.	Supplies	1,000
4.	Phone	2,000
5.	Postage	300
	Subtotal	$ 7,800

TRAVEL

1.	20,000 miles @ 21¢/mile	$ 4,200
2.	40 lodging nights @ $27.50	1,100
3.	Meals	2,000
	Subtotal	$ 7,300

MATERIALS

1.	Brochure production, 500 copies, 2 color, line art	$ 225
2.	Letterhead stationery, 1,000 envelopes and letters	50
3.	Newsletter, 1 issue, printing 400 copies, folding, collating, stock paper	100
	Subtotal	$ 375
	TOTAL	$77,865

a newsletter for all owners of significant areas and at least annual visits, just to stay in touch and to monitor the status of the property.

Summary

More elements of natural diversity are destroyed through ignorance than through malice. Notifying a landowner that something special occurs on his property and discovering his attitude toward the information can be a prelude to stronger protection. The information should contain a credible statement based on a comprehensive statewide inventory of the relative significance of the population, community, or species that occurs on his property. The information is ideally imparted by a nonthreatening program representative in an informal atmosphere.

APPENDIX A

Sample Letter of Introduction

October 1, 1980

Mr. Forest E. Canopy
RFD 1
Pallor, Transylvania 52761

Dear Mr. Canopy,

For the past three years the Transylvania Natural Heritage Program has been conducting an inventory to identify the best remaining examples of the native plants and animals and communities of vegetation remaining in our state. Researchers have found that you are the owner of an excellent bottomland hardwood forest, of a type that was once widespread throughout the Transylvania River Basin.

I would like to talk with you about the forest, mainly to discuss its history and present condition. I will be contacting you in the near future to arrange a convenient time when I might visit you for a few minutes.

The Transylvania Nature Conservancy, which I represent, is a nonprofit, nongovernmental organization which works to preserve the remnants of our state's natural heritage for the benefit of future generations. I look forward to speaking with you.

Sincerely,

Director

CHAPTER SIX

REGISTRATION

A registry is a credible list of important things, an honor roll of special members whose very excellence begs for constructive attention. If registrants happen to be natural areas, it is possible to protect them by controlling the extent to which they can be developed (if the legal authority exists), or by recognizing and rewarding their owners just as students are often rewarded when they find themselves on a scholastic honor roll.

A "credible" list does not necessarily mean an official list. Private organizations, or individuals for that matter, can create their own registries. The Bowater Timber Company, for example, has registered certain of its most remote inholdings as "pocket wildernesses" and has opened these tracts for passive public use. By doing so, Bowater has drawn considerable attention and benefited the informed public. A registry is most credible if criteria are precise and the selection process is rigorous. The relative significance of every site on a meaningful registry is supported by solid data.

The Federal Endangered Species Program, the National Natural Landmark Program, and the National Register of Historic Places are examples of the many public programs that are organized around a list of significant entities. Sometimes the enabling law restricts or regulates development of the areas listed. For instance, the National Historic Preservation Act requires sponsors of projects needing federal funds, permits, or licenses to consider the project's potential effect upon any of the more than 16,000 entries on the National Register of Historic Places. When conflicts arise, the Advisory Council on Historic Preservation confers with the project sponsor to seek ways of lessening the impact on the registered place.

Registry programs can also influence development indirectly. For example, the sponsor of a proposed project that might threaten a National Natural Landmark could be required to prepare an environmental impact statement under the National Environmental Policy Act,[1] even though no law directly relating to the landmark program would compel him to do so.

It is becoming increasingly difficult, however, to regulate development through registries. State legislatures and Congress are shying away from land use regulation in general and seem especially chary of regulation that might affect all the items on open-ended lists, such as the federal list of endangered species. Registries appear to possess limited strength as purely regulatory devices, but they can also be used creatively in other ways.

Voluntary Programs: A Recognition Model

A number of states have decided to use the registration concept not to regulate development, but rather to encourage landowners to volunteer to protect the natural elements that occur on their property. In simple terms the owner agrees in writing to protect specific features and receives a symbol—such as a plaque or certificate—recognizing the significance of the property and his contribution to an overall effort to preserve his state's natural heritage. The agreement is nonbinding, is given freely, and does not affect the deed (see Appendix A). It has no legal force, and the owner can back out at any time. The approach is all carrot and no stick.

As of January 1980, about 15 states had the legal authority to conduct registries of natural areas, and of those about 11 are at least preparing recognition programs. Enabling language is usually indefinite; the legislators give few clues as to what a registry actually is. They just tell you to set one up. Here are two typical examples:

> The Department . . . shall establish and maintain a registry of natural areas of unusual significance.　　　　　　　　　　　　　　(Ohio)[2]

> In order to give recognition to natural areas, the Department shall establish and maintain a registry of natural areas of unusual significance. . . .　　　　　　　　　　　　　　　　　　　(Indiana)[3]

Essentially, these provisions obligate the state only to keep a list, which is exactly what most states do at first. Until recently Ohio had file folders full of information on over 500 areas that had at one time or another caught the attention of members of the Ohio Biological Survey. Now state officials have begun to use Ohio heritage program data to separate wheat from chaff and to devise a landowner recognition program.

For the sake of funding and continuity it is helpful if a registry is established by law, but it is not imperative. The North Carolina Department of Natural Resources and Community Development established a program in 1979 through an administrative rule.

Incentives to Landowners

A recognition-type registry program doesn't seem very powerful at face value. Indeed, the landowner seems to be giving something up by agreeing not to cut or plow, drain or fill, but he doesn't appear to be getting much of anything in return. Where is the cash or tax shelter? After all, land speculators circle undeveloped property like vultures these days.

Anyone who decides to conduct a registry program has to figure out how to provide attractive incentives for participation in a voluntary program. Here are some ways to accentuate the positive.

Emphasize the Owner's Generosity and Civic-mindedness. You are soliciting an act of volunteerism. Don't make the agreement letter too official, legal-looking, or severe, and don't send it by registered mail. Forget the henceforths and thereofs. The owner should feel obligated to restrict his activities in specific ways that are provided in the agreement, but his obligation is moral, not legal. The real power of this concept is pride. The landowner is proud that his property contains an Ohio Natural Landmark or North Carolina Heritage Landmark, and proud of himself for having rendered a civic gesture. He has agreed to do something that will help preserve Indiana's natural heritage and deserves the gratitude of fellow Hoosiers.

Offer to publicize the act of registration, but don't insist if the owner seems at all shy about it. Landowners who have objected to the registration of their property have frequently stated as a reason their belief that the location of their property will be publicized. You are publicizing the owner's gesture, not his property.

Reward Him Impressively. If the owner's reward is to be largely symbolic, it had better be impressive. Don't trim the budget here. A good-looking symbol can sometimes be more compelling than any verbal statement you can make. For example, the director of the North Carolina Natural Heritage Registry Program recalls a rural gentleman who cut him off in the middle of an extended appeal by saying, "Okay, I'll take a plaque."

Indiana has elected to give each registrant a handsome walnut plaque in the shape of the state. Owners of significant tracts in Delaware receive a volume with a permanent feel to it called *Delaware's Outstanding Natural Areas and Their Preservation*,[4] which retailed in 1978 for about $17. If you decide to offer a certificate, use good parchment, frame it, and affix close to the landowner's name the most notable signature you can find.

53

When a landowner looks up from a good book, Ol' Blue at his feet and a blaze in the hearth, his eyes should be drawn to a solid reminder of the worth of his land and his stature as a citizen.

North Carolina Registry of Natural Heritage Areas

This is to certify that the

North Carolina Department of Natural Resources and Community Development has found

in the ownership of

to include highly significant natural features and to be critical to the preservation of North Carolina's natural diversity.

As a result of this finding and for the purposes of recognition and protection this area is officially included on the

Registry of Natural Heritage Areas

_____
Secretary, Department of Natural Resources & Community Development

_____
Date

Certificate awarded to owners of registered natural areas in North Carolina.

Send the Right Person to Meet Him. It is important that a courteous and credible spokesperson introduce the program to the landowner. This was discussed at length in the previous chapter, and it holds true for any negotiating strategy. In many instances a representative of a private organization may be the best person to ask a landowner to refrain voluntarily from developing certain areas. A spokesperson for the Interior Department's National Natural Landmarks Program cites distrust of the federal government as the reason most frequently given by landowners who have refused to register their property.[5] (This issue can be exaggerated— approximately 80 percent of all owners of eligible landmark properties have agreed to register.) Still, perhaps especially in the West, private representatives might be more successful. Partly for this reason Indiana has decided to weld together a three-party registry program. Funded by a private foundation grant, potential registry sites are first identified by data provided primarily by the Indiana heritage program, then screened for eligibility by the Indiana Division of Nature Preserves. Finally, landowners are contacted by a Nature Conservancy representative.

Offer Management Advice and Assistance. Many generous and public-spirited citizens are delighted to learn that their property contains a population of plants, a prairie remnant, or a heron rookery, but they don't know what to do next. Some are a little intimidated by this knowledge. Some common reactions include: "Do I leave it alone, or what?" "How can I tell if they're doing all right?" "If something goes wrong, whom do I contact?"

An offer of assistance and advice in managing the elements of concern can be a relief to the owner and a further incentive to cooperate. The offer can also backfire if it presents to a skeptical landowner an early play for control of his property, a "foot in the door." Management assistance should be an offer rather than a requirement (although Georgia can claim some success with its registry program, which requires landowners to agree to formal master plans).[6] A clear management plan for each registered property would be ideal. There should also be a person for the owner to call if something bad (or good) happens.

Sources of management assistance have not been fully explored. For instance, in 1976 the Soil Conservation Service amended its administrative regulations to include natural areas within the scope of its extension services.[7] Most extension agents are not trained scientists, but they do know the land, people, and land use patterns within their territories. Workshops involving different extension agencies could increase their ability to help registrants.

Consider the Use of Financial Incentives. It is possible for state or local jurisdictions to sweeten the pot for registrants by reducing the assessed value of their properties because they have agreed not to develop it to its full potential. Such arrangements have been applied throughout the country to promote the preservation of forests and croplands, but have probably never been used to protect natural areas.

However, there are some promising signs. The Indiana General Assembly recently passed a bill providing for a reduced assessment to owners of certain kinds of wildlife habitat.[8] The program administrator views "wildlife" broadly enough to include rare plant habitats and would consider extending the offer to owners of registered Indiana natural areas. Likewise, Tennessee has considered intermittently a reduced assessment under the Tennessee Agriculture, Forest and Open Space Act of 1976 for owners of properties listed on the Tennessee Natural Heritage Registry.

Two notes of caution: First, these preferential assessment schemes, as they are known, have not been uniformly successful. Usually the statute provides that a landowner who backs out of the program at a certain point in order to sell or develop his property has to pay "roll back" taxes equal to the total value of the reduction received over the years. That penalty has not been enough to keep landowners from yielding to speculative offers; in fact, buyers routinely factor the roll back into the purchase price. The term of the roll back has to be long for the provision to be meaningful.

Secondly, the reduced assessment is not always granted automatically, nor is its value always substantial. It is up to the owner to apply— sometimes persistently—for the reduction. Some assessors oppose reduced assessments because they view it as a raid on the revenue base or as a plain headache. This issue is discussed at length in Chapter Ten.

Stay in Touch. The brightest of plaques tarnish in time, parchment yellows, and even heavy volumes are misplaced. Every cooperating landowner should be reminded periodically that the program still exists, that its sponsors still care (personally), that his contribution is remembered and valued. Again, the best reminders are visits, brochures, and newsletters. Perhaps a wall calendar could serve as a constant reminder.

Keep Track of Information and Monitor Your Progress

Registry programs, like landowner notification programs, enable you to meet the owners of hundreds of property tracts. This is a major advantage for ark-builders, but it's hard to keep track of the status of your efforts when you're dealing with so many owners, particularly if there are several transactions involved with each (the letter, the phone call, the visit, the reaction, the next call, designing and mailing a plaque, and so forth).

In Indiana, workers use a checklist of elements of the state's natural diversity, as compiled by scientists within the state for the Indiana Natural Area Registry Program (see Appendix B). The list, which is alphabetized by element class (plants, animals, and community types), displays in tabular form the relative urgency of registering an example right away (an element that is protected at least twice on an Indiana nature preserve is assigned a secondary priority) and shows the current status of the attempt to register a good occurrence. The checklist is updated continually.

The Indiana program has also designed a "Tract Visit Summary" (see Appendix C), which its sole field representative fills out in a few minutes after each visit. The information required allows him to characterize the owners and their attitudes and to prepare for the next step.

Regulation and Recognition

If the natural elements on a registry can be protected both because their listing inhibits development and because landowners have agreed to protect them, an interesting question arises: If you are running the registry program, do you list eligible features before the landowner consents to protect them or even despite his objections (indeed, they are the most important features in the state, no matter what the owner thinks); or do you list them only with the owner's blessing (he might destroy them or sue you if he finds out they've been listed without his permission)?

It is probably better to list areas only with the owner's consent. Mere listing is not a particularly powerful gesture in the first place since the state usually has no direct authority to regulate development of registered properties. Besides, credible data demonstrating the relative significance of a natural feature can trigger indirect regulation through impact assessments, whether a property is listed or not.

For instance, suppose a developer has to apply for federal funds and/or approval, and the heritage program in his state has an opportunity to comment on the project as described in an A-95 Bulletin (see Chapter Thirteen). The developer will sooner or later learn something like "One of four colonies of *Geum radiatum* known to occur in the state has been reported at a place that appears to be on your proposed development site." At an early stage, when the developer can still change his plans easily, this information would probably be just as compelling as "Your project will threaten a Mississippi Natural Landmark unless you adjust your plans." The landmark status merely adds lustre to an already substantial statement.

Of course it is always possible that an unhappy landowner could sue the state, claiming that listing represented a taking without compensation or encumbered his property without consent. With such claims in mind, the solicitor for the Department of the Interior[9] has advised natural registry program sponsors to notify landowners prior to listing the features on their properties.

There is no evidence that registration encumbers property or deflates property values. A 1979 study found that designation of properties as critical areas in Maine has no effect on property values, marketability of the land, or on the decision to buy or sell the property. A few owners of properties that have been listed on the National Register of Historic Places have filed suit claiming that registration is a taking of property since it makes the property more difficult to sell for development purposes. The taking claim has never succeeded in court.[10]

On the brighter side there is much to be gained in approaching the landowner before listing the area. The owner's cooperation now may lead to stronger protection later. He may be able to help promote the program to other landowners. If he agrees to protect the area, he will probably allow it to be listed anyway.

Registration and Other Protection Tools

A registry program is most useful as part of a system of protection tools. A nonbinding, voluntary agreement is ideal as either a foothold or as a fallback position. Voluntary registration is an important stride beyond notification because the landowner has agreed to protect the natural elements on his property. He has made at least a psychological commitment. Registration is a good fallback option to use when negotiating with landowners who are simply not willing to part with any of the rights to their property but who care about its natural significance.

A registry of natural areas should include only the most significant areas in its universe. The relative significance of every area on the list should be readily demonstrable. Decisionmakers and landowners are influenced by a registry only if they believe that the list contains only true nuggets, patiently sifted from streams of biological information. If insignificant areas are listed, they cheapen the currency. The list and the listers will not be trusted.

Case Study:
The Maine Critical Areas Registry

There is no textbook state registration program in the United States. Several of the programs exist only in design form; and the Indiana and North Carolina programs, both off to fine starts, are still too new to be conclusive. Others seem to be struggling for definition as either a recognition or regulatory program.

Perhaps the Maine Critical Areas Program (MCAP)[11] is the most instructive of all, partly because it is the best established of all state registration programs—having registered well over 200 areas since its inception—partly because the staff has kept statistical records throughout the program's history and is thus able to measure its performance and partly because the enabling statute gives us a model to avoid.

Even though MCAP is not in essence a voluntary program (landowners are not asked to sign voluntary protection agreements), it is similar in style to such programs. MCAP almost never registers property without a landowner's consent, and the process of persuading a landowner that registration of his property is a good thing is similar to persuading a landowner to sign a protection agreement; pride and recognition are the prime incentives. MCAP awards framable certificates to owners of critical areas, and management assistance is offered.

The MCAP was established by an act of legislature in 1974. The act provided for an inventory of areas possessing unusual natural, scenic, scientific, or historic importance and established procedures for their listing as "critical" areas. MCAP is conducted entirely by the state, through the State Planning Office, with advice and assistance from an 11-member advisory board appointed by the governor.

Most of the day-to-day administration of the program—including subcontracting for inventory work, preparing promotional materials, keeping program records, and landowner relations — is conducted by one indefatigable worker, assisted by whatever interns he can attract and fund. The board's primary role has been to consider the wisdom of registering sites recommended as eligible by the inventory. In the best of New England traditions, they have deliberated these matters at public meetings, to which affected landowners have been invited. MCAP's $46,000 operating budget for 1979 derived from a $23,000 state appropriation, matched by a Coastal Zone Management and Water Resources grant.

MCAP is like the Illinois Landowner Contact Program in that it begins by inventorying sectors of the landscape, evaluates data to determine which areas are significant enough for further attention, finds out who owns the priority areas, and notifies the owners. It is with notification that the similarity ends.

A Formal Process of Notification. In one sense the legislature denied those conducting the program the best features of both regulation and recognition. The act provides for formal notification in the style of public notice for a permit hearing, with receipt of a registered letter triggering a 60-day comment period, after which time a public meeting is convened to consider an issue. But the issue at stake — to register or not to register — carries no real regulatory implication. The owner of a registered property is obligated only to notify the state before altering a registered feature. He can go ahead and alter it, he just has to tell the state. In effect the staff has no carrot to offer landowners, but a twig to brandish at potential developers.

Because a registered letter can be a chilly introduction, staff members have redrafted the introductory letter many times to soften its tone and clarify its message. At worst, a landowner can feel that something has already happened to his land, that an inexorable process has begun, and that in about two months the merits of his property will be discussed in public. Furthermore, even though he has two months to vent his feelings, it looks like this "registration" can happen no matter what he says.

MCAP and Landowner Relations. Despite the formality imposed by the enabling legislation, the program has been successful. The staff has not been content to wait for a formal response to their notification letter, but has instead followed up quickly with phone calls, visits, and additional written material. They persuade by informing, and their informational material is impressive. They have been patient and open with landowners, have kept records of their experiences, and have thus been able to refine their approaches. Table 1 is a summary of response to the initial MCAP notification letter and the initial attitude toward registration of landowners of 234 registered critical areas.

The staff's attempt to characterize the landowner's attitude toward registration is admittedly subjective. There are many shades of gray between "mildly positive" and "very positive." Still, a supportive trend is indicated.

Table 1—Landowners' Response to Notification

RESPONSES OF LANDOWNER	NUMBER OF RESPONSES	PERCENT
Responded in writing	122	52
Called Critical Areas Program office	3	1
Staff called landowner regarding the area	166	71
Number of landowners visited by staff	56	24
ATTITUDE OF LANDOWNER		
Apathetic	42	18
Mildly positive	88	38
Very positive	84	36
Initially objected	17	7
MCAP registered over objection	2	1

The board and staff have also decided not to register areas if the landowner objects strenuously. (They have registered areas only twice over a landowner's objection.) This has not meant that they've taken the first — sometimes reflexive — "no" for an answer. MCAP has frequently entered into prolonged negotiations with landowners and their attorneys. Objections usually fall into one or more of seven broad categories.

The landowner questions the accuracy of the data. This has not been a major problem. The critical areas inventory is painstakingly methodical and thorough. Field surveys are contracted element by element, a very few at a time. Maine finds out, for example, where all of its active common eider nests are located, then selects the best as eligible for registration. All sites have been visited recently, and if the owner doubts the data, a staffer shows the owner where the element occurs, usually in the company of the original surveyor.

The landowner questions mapped boundaries. Usually a joint perusal of available maps can work out the kinks. Sometimes the owner produces a better map.

The landowner wants to develop the land or build a structure in the future. Only a few times have construction plans really menaced a proposed critical area. Usually some acceptable compromise can be fashioned.

The owner fears that registration will affect the value of his property. This issue has been raised frequently. The staff routinely responds that there is no evidence that registration has resulted in decreased property values. During 1977 and 1978 title transfers took place on at least ten registered critical areas. MCAP staffers do not believe that critical area designation reduced the value of any of these properties or complicated their transfers. In a number of cases registration had a positive influence on the transfer. The Nature Conservancy acquired two registered areas, and the State of Maine acquired two registered areas.[12]

The landowner fears that registration means the state will regulate his property. Concerns of this nature usually take the form of implying that a government program will lead to further government regulation and denial of private property rights. The staff attempts to convince the owner that the program is nonregulatory in nature.

Landowners fear publicity. Landowners are concerned that information about their properties will be made public. In responding, the staff notes the MCAP policy of not even considering publicity unless the landowner so requests. Some examples of the few areas that have been publicized are well-known areas in federal or state parks and Nature Conservancy preserves. No landowner has yet complained to MCAP that registration has resulted in publicity of his property.

The owner fears that registration will lead to government condemnation. The staff responds that the State Planning Office has no power to acquire land. It is also noted that the state buys very little land, mainly because there is little money to do so.

Follow-Up. Continued contact with landowners is especially important in Maine because the enabling legislation requires owners of registered critical areas to notify the board at least 60 days before altering a registered feature. Since the act imposes no burden of compliance and no penalties for violation, it's mainly up to the staff to carry out this provision by maintaining the relationship.

They do so primarily through questionnaires. Ironically, when they ask if there has been a change in the critical area, they may be asking the owner to admit he has broken a law.

In November 1978 questionnaires were sent to the landowners of the first 128 registered critical areas. A postage-paid, self-addressed postcard was enclosed so the landowners could easily answer questions regarding changes in the registered areas and changes in ownership. Owners of 112 areas (88 percent) responded. There was a change in ownership in only 9 areas (7 percent), and a contemplated change of ownership in 1979 for 3 areas. The program has notified the five new landowners about the significance of the critical area they recently acquired. Changes took place in one area because of a fire, and in a second area because of winter storm erosion.

MCAP and the Illinois Landowner Contact Program

Finally, it is interesting to compare MCAP to the Illinois Landowner Contact Program. Both begin as broad-based notification programs, advising hundreds of people, often for the first time, that there is something special on their property. But Illinois enjoys the luxury of an unstressed first encounter. Illinois uses the contact program as a basis for obtaining information from which to formulate subsequent protection strategies, which may include registration. It is probably wise to be prepared to negotiate a protection agreement on the first meeting should the opportunity arise, but it is also probably a mistake to *have* to do something the first time out.

Summary

A registry is a formal list of special things, which can be occurrences of natural elements. The list, if the legal power exists, can be used to regulate development of targeted properties. The registry can also be used to recognize property owners who agree voluntarily to protect elements of natural diversity. In working with a voluntary registration model, the appearance and quality of the symbols selected to recognize a landowner's generosity and the significance of his property are very important. It is also important to maintain continual contact with each registrant.

APPENDIX A

Model Letter of Agreement to Register and Protect
a State Natural Heritage Area

I, __Vladimir Badinoff__ , owner of the area known as __Melancholy Slough__ agree to allow the area described and bounded on the enclosed map to be registered as a Transylvania Natural Heritage Area. I agree not to take any intentional action which could destroy or degrade the heritage area so long as the property is registered.

I agree to allow qualified representatives of the Department of Natural Resources to visit the property from time to time to examine the condition of the heritage area and the natural elements within. Should I observe any significant change in the condition of the heritage area or any of the elements within, I agree to notify the Department of Natural Resources. Should the apparent change be adverse, I agree to allow an effort, conducted at the department's expense, to restore the area to its full health.

I agree to notify the department at least 45 days before I transfer by any means the title to the registered property or decide for any reason to withdraw from this agreement.

I, __Janet L. Miasma__ , director of the Transylvania Department of Natural Resources, hereby register for an indefinite period __Melancholy Slough__ . This agreement can be terminated in writing by either party, giving 45 days notice.

It is understood that this agreement involves no change of title, or loss of ownership rights, but simply expresses the landowner's sincere intention to protect certain natural elements of statewide significance and the department's desire to recognize the importance of his property and his civic gesture by awarding him a plaque. Neither party shall incur any liability for any injury to persons or property on the land.

By_____   By_____
   Owner   Director

APPENDIX B

Plant Communities
Partial Checklist of Elements Used by Indiana Natural Area Registry Program

Element	No. of Protected Occurrences	Priority for Registry	Registry Status	Action Indicated
☐ Quercus coccinea - Quercus alba	0	A	Abbott's Hollow nominated - on hold	Nominate Beaver Bend
☐ Quercus - Alnus - Fraxinus	1	C	—	Nominate Davis Forestry Farm
☐ Quercus muhlenbergii - Quercus rubra	0	A	—	Nominate Muscatatuck River Bluffs
☐ Quercus palustris	0	A	NEED MORE INFORMATION	
☐ Quercus palustris - Liquidambar styriciflua	0	A	—	Nominate Corner Woods
☐ Quercus prinus	0	A	Letter written 5/7/80	Find another site
☐ Quercus prinus - Castanea dentata	NEED INFORMATION			
☐ Quercus rubra - Acer saccharum	2	D	Allee Woods registered	
☐ Quercus rubra - Acer saccharum - Tilia americana	2	D	—	
☐ Quercus rubra - Quercus alba	0	A	—	Nominate High Bridge Way Dunning Woods
☐ Quercus shumardii - Carya laciniosa	0	A	Kramer Woods nominated	Cave Woods
☐ Quercus stellata	0	A	Half Moon Woods SR	Nominate Cypress Slough Posey
☐ Quercus velutina	1	C	NO SITES	

KEY: A = Top priority B = Site registered C = Element with one protected occurrence D = Two or more protected occurrences

APPENDIX C

Indiana Natural Areas Registry

How does the Indiana Natural Areas Registry work?

Here are the answers to some basic questions about the program:

- ## Who operates the Registry?

  The Indiana Natural Areas Registry was created by the Indiana Nature Conservancy and the Indiana Department of Natural Resources. The Nature Conservancy is a private nonprofit conservation group established in Indiana in 1959 to help protect natural areas. Its 2,000 members have established 50 preserves by purchase or gift. The Department of Natural Resources (D.N.R.) traces its beginnings to Colonel Lieber, who in the early 1900's acquired Turkey Run, Spring Mill, McCormick's Creek, Clifty Falls, Brown County Park, and The Dunes. In 1979, the Lilly Endowment of Indianapolis provided the funds for the Registry, which enables the Conservancy and the D.N.R. to jointly recognize the contributions made by Hoosier citizens in protecting our state's natural legacy.

White lady's slipper.
Threatened in Indiana

- ## How does an area qualify for the Registry?

  To qualify as an Indiana natural area eligible for registration, a property must contain one or more of these natural values:
  1) habitat for plants or animals with declining populations in Indiana;
  2) plant communities characteristic of the native vegetation of Indiana;
  3) outstanding natural features such as virgin forests or bogs.

- ## How does inclusion on the Registry protect a natural area?

  Registration effectively encourages conservation of important natural lands in private or public ownership. By informing landowners of the uniqueness of particular sites, registration reduces the chance that significant natural values may be unwittingly destroyed. The same recognition will discourage others, such as governmental agencies and utilities, from disturbing the area.

- ## What say does the landowner have in the registration process?

  The registration of a natural area is totally up to the landowner and will not occur without his or her approval.

- ## What recognition does a property-owner receive for including his or her land on the Registry?

- **Is the commitment binding on the owner of a registered natural area?**

  No. The commitment may be cancelled by the landowner at any time, although he or she is asked to give 30-days' notice before terminating the registration. If the owner fails to protect an area, the director of the D.N.R. Division of Nature Preserves may remove the area from the Registry, and the owner will be asked to return the plaque.

- **Are there financial advantages for registering a natural area?**

  Registration involves no payment or receipt of funds. Local tax officials may wish to consider the registration of a natural area when determining the property's use value, but they are not bound to do so. The Registry director will provide information on a variety of other programs—classified forest, classified wildlife habitat, conservation easement, bargain sale and gift—that can offer significant tax savings to the landowner.

Yellowwood
Endangered in Indiana

- **Does registration of a site permit public access to private property?**

  No. Registration of a natural area provides no rights of public access to a private property. As with any private land, visitors must receive permission from the landowner before entering the property.

- **Is management assistance available to the owner of a registered area?**

  Yes. An owner of a registered area may receive management advice from the Division of Nature Preserves. When sufficient staff expertise is unavailable, outside assistance will be sought.

Drawings by William Zimmerman

Bobcat
Endangered in Indiana

Without the commitment and concern of individual landowners, we stand to lose, year by year, portions of our rich natural heritage. The Indiana Natural Areas Registry is citizen-based conservation —and citizenship is an Indiana tradition.

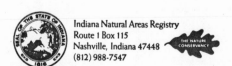

Indiana Natural Areas Registry
Route 1 Box 115
Nashville, Indiana 47448
(812) 988-7547

APPENDIX D

Trip Report Form Used by Indiana Natural Registry Program

Indiana Natural Area Registry　　　　　　　Date: _____

TRACT VISIT SUMMARY

Site name, if any:　　　　　　　　　　　Primary tract_____
　　　　　　　　　　　　　　　　　　　　Secondary tract_____

Tract owner(s):

Narrative account of visit:

Age of owner(s):

How long has owner owned tract?

How is the tract used now?

Owner(s) occupation:

Children:
How many?_____　　　Ages (Range): _____

Was owner aware of target occurrence?
Yes_____　　　　　　No_____

Did (s)he realize that they were important?
Yes_____　　　　　　No_____

Had (s)he protected them deliberately?
Yes_____　　　　　　No_____

Owner(s) attitude toward new information:
Interest_____　　Indifference_____　　Pleased_____　　Antagonism_____

Owner(s) attitude toward registration:
Positive_____　　Uncertain_____　　Requested time_____　　Negative_____

Did owner express attitude toward state?_____　Characterize:

Did owner express attitude toward TNC?_____　Characterize:

Owner(s) apparent desire re tract: (Check more than one, if appropriate)
Short-term income_____　　　　　　Hedge against inflation_____
Means of subsistence_____　　　　　Link to tradition, past_____
Place for children_____　　　　　　Place to live_____
Spiritual, aesthetic values_____　　Other_____(Characterize):

Present plans for property:

Estimated dollar value of tract: _____

Threats to occurrences, if any:
Immediate:　　　　　　　　　　　　　Long range:

Action re registry indicated by visit:

CHAPTER SEVEN

DESIGNATION OF PUBLIC LANDS

About 40 percent of all land in the United States is publicly owned. Someone wishing to protect elements of Nevada's or Idaho's or Alaska's natural diversity will have to look hard to find private landowners with whom to negotiate. Even though most land held by public agencies is used for recreation, forestry, and agriculture, most agencies can "designate," or set aside for specific conservation purposes, the lands they manage through their own administrative processes.

Most agencies have several designation categories. For example, the U.S. Forest Service can designate an area harboring "authentic, significant, and interesting evidence of our American natural heritage as it pertains to fauna" as a Special Interest Zoological Area[1] or a "botanical" area containing "significant plant specimens, populations, or communities" as a Special Interest Botanical Area.[2]

The vast majority of all public land in the United States is owned by the federal government and controlled by the following five major landholding agencies:

1. The National Park Service
2. The Department of Defense
3. The U.S. Fish and Wildlife Service
4. The Bureau of Land Management
5. The U.S. Forest Service

Each of these agencies and many others have several programs that could be used to protect significant natural elements. Some programs have been established by Congress and involve both Congress and the general public throughout the designation process. For instance, most areas within the National Wildlife Refuge System, administered by the U.S. Fish and Wildlife Service, were acquired through money appropriated by Congress.

By contrast, "Public Use Natural Areas" are designated by the service's administrators — without public or congressional involvement — to preserve:

...relatively undisturbed ecosystem(s) or sub-ecosystems that can be enjoyed by the public under certain restrictions without destroying (them).[3]

There are also many state designation programs. For instance, the Hawaii Department of Land and Natural Resources can designate its own holdings as "natural area preserves."

This chapter will not attempt to catalog the various natural area conservation programs available within each major public agency. That information is available, current as of October 31, 1975, in two encyclopedic volumes entitled *Preserving Our Natural Heritage*,[4] prepared for the Department of the Interior by The Nature Conservancy. Volume I describes federal agencies and programs, while Volume II discusses the efforts of state governments to protect ecologically significant areas. Both volumes are thoroughly researched, full of case studies, and remain very useful even though some programs have changed and some agencies have been reorganized.

Hundreds of administrative designations have been created, but just because they exist does not mean they are used. Programs launched in a fever of enthusiasm have a way of being left to cool. There are plenty of natural areas "systems" with one or two areas.

There are understandable reasons for this. A resource manager has a lot on his mind. His agency's administrative regulations may provide for designation of natural areas; but unit plans, policy directives, and legal obligations seize his immediate attention. For instance, a forest supervisor is apt to be pressured to meet forestwide timber quotas, harvesting, and marketing goals; to control fires, pests, and diseases; to keep hillsides from sliding into streams; to lease grazing land; balance the books; increase his budget; and keep the public happy. He may employ a forest biologist, or even an endangered species specialist, but he may not know from day to day whether natural elements occur in his forest, whether he or one of his predecessors has already protected them, and if not, whether he can do anything to protect them. Furthermore, his awareness of these matters should not depend upon a personal relationship with an informed individual since that person is likely to be working at a different national forest in two or three years.

Strength of Protection

Most designation programs are created administratively rather than by

72

a legislative body. The programs thus have no force of law, except in the broad sense that the ability to make administrative regulations has a basis in law. Should the managers of a national forest decide that an area once designated as a "Special Interest Botanical Area" because it contained a population of rare plants is suddenly more valuable to the forest as a grazing area, they can withdraw the designation arbitrarily. There is no elaborate chain of command or public review process.

Some designated natural areas protected by federal agencies—most notably by the Bureau of Land Management—are "withdrawn" from uses permitted under conflicting land laws such as the mineral leasing law, which permits leasing of gas, oil, coal, and phosphate. Withdrawal strengthens protection by limiting the use of land to specific purposes, such as the protection of natural elements that could otherwise be jeopardized by claims made under various land laws.

Both Congress and the president can withdraw lands. The process of withdrawal is born (at least for the Bureau of Land Management) with a request for permission to file an application, passes through a prolonged pupal stage in the Department of Interior's hierarchy, and emerges as a public land order.

Probably the best designation programs—the programs that will probably endure—are those that set aside carefully selected places, each contributing to a clearly defined system of preserves in order to fulfill a specific objective. In such a system one could measure the loss of any component. A U.S. Fish and Wildlife Service property that has been designated a Research Natural Area (RNA) has no greater legal protection than if it were designated as a "Public Use Natural Area." Either way, the service could change its use status. But because an RNA is part of an effort now involving eight federal agencies, which has existed since 1927, administrators might be less likely to sacrifice an RNA to another land use.

The RNA objective is clear—to preserve a representative array of all significant ecosystems on federal lands as baseline research areas—even if no common inventory focuses the program. There might be some peer, institutional, even moral pressure working on behalf of a Research Natural Area absent from a program more recently established by a single agency.

To cite one example of an institutional incentive for designation, the U.S. Fish and Wildlife Service's "Recreational Benefit Unit" (RBU) Refuge Point system rewards refuges which contain designated Research Natural Areas. The RBU system was established to enable resource managers to compare the productivity of individual refuges, as related to agency goals. Refuges receive RBUs for about 30 different values, including waterfowl production (breeding) and waterfowl use (a refuge gets 800 RBU points whenever a duck spends a day there). The point incentives for designation of Research Natural Areas are sufficiently strong to bolster a refuge's chances of receiving funds for construction projects or staff additions.

In the two case studies below, one manager decided to designate inholdings because he became aware that there were significant elements within his domain, the other because mapped data convinced him that he could protect something precious without impeding his program.

Case Study:
The Boardman Bombing Range

The U.S. Navy's Boardman Bombing Range had been surveyed by members of the Oregon Natural Area Preserves Advisory Committee (ONAPAC) around 1975. The Boardman data were incorporated into the Oregon Natural Heritage Program (ONHP) data base about a year later.

Early in 1978 a heritage staff ecologist read a newspaper article stating that much of the Boardman Range had been leased out for grazing. A navy spokesman stated in the article that much of the range was not needed for bombing maneuvers and grazing seemed a good use of excess land.

The ecologist drove to the office and discovered that several element occurrences had been recorded on the Boardman site. He believed the site to be important enough to warrant designation as a Research Natural Area.

His task was to persuade the navy itself to make the designation, since a participating federal agency can establish an RNA only through its own administrative processes. The ecologist decided to try from the bottom up, first contacting the navy land stewards. Working with the chairman of the State Natural Area Preserves Advisory Committee, he first contacted the civilian forester in charge of grazing and forestry in the Pacific Northwest. The forester's name was found on the "source of lead" column on the heritage program data transcription form for several of the element occurrences since he had been contacted by the original ONAPAC surveyors.

The forester listened to the ecologist's presentation, which was based largely upon the presence at Boardman of several rare animal species and a threatened grassland type. Finally he said, somewhat annoyed, "Why

74

didn't you tell me about this sooner? I've already leased it out." Undaunt-
ed, the ecologist persisted in his appeal and finally persuaded the forester
to look at the land with him. The forester's eventual enthusiasm for protecting the land proved instrumental to the designation.

The problem shifted to how to designate land already leased for grazing. The forester contacted the navy grazing manager and explained the
situation, offering to show the grazing manager the points of interest on
the land. Shortly thereafter the ecologist, the ONAPAC chairman, the
forester, the grazing manager, the lessee, and several university scientists
spent two days together on the land. The scientists pointed out very specific areas for protection. The field experience seemed to excite everyone,
and by the end of the second day there was general agreement that several
specific areas should be withdrawn from the lease and that an effort
would be made to designate those sites as RNAs. The heritage ecologist
and two other plant ecologists spent the next three days conducting an intensive field survey at Boardman collecting data that could be used to jus-
tify the RNA designation.

The next step was the most important. The base commander, a navy
captain, would make the final RNA decision, and he had not yet been ap-
proached. Before making a formal proposal, the grazing manager visited
the commander and discussed the idea with him generally. He left a summary of the site analysis the ecologists had written and arranged a formal
meeting. The grazing manager assured the commander that normal mili-
tary procedures would not be interrupted by the designation. In retrospect, the ecologist believes the commander had already made up his mind
before the first formal meeting.

Before formally approaching the commander, the ecologist sought the
assistance of experienced land negotiators. He met with two Nature Conservancy representatives and with a representative of the Pacific Northwest
RNA Committee to prepare an effective presentation.

They met with the commander several weeks later. After listening to
the formal RNA proposal, the commander again sought—and received
—assurances that the designation would not interfere with bombing
maneuvers. He gave his verbal approval and expressed the hope that the
designation would give the navy some good press.

The ecologist then presented the complete ecological justification in

75

writing to the Pacific Northwest RNA Committee and requested designation. He received almost immediate verbal approval, and the Boardman Bombing Range has been designated a Research Natural Area (see Appendix A).

Case Study:
The Santiago Oak Savannah
Research Natural Area

The Minnesota chapter of The Nature Conservancy (TNC) had for several years been looking for a good example of an oak savannah. A true oak savannah—a prairie supporting widely scattered bur, northern pin, and red oak trees—is a rare and sensitive ecosystem. It was a fairly extensive system before the country was settled, but once settlers began to subdue the wildfires that maintained the savannahs, most of them either phased into forests or were plowed.

In June 1978 a TNC student intern looking for examples of blue lupine, an uncommon plant in Minnesota, visited the Sherburne National Wildlife Refuge, managed by the U.S. Fish and Wildlife Service. He found there not only a large colony of blue lupine, but also a 300-acre oak savannah along a river floodplain. Ironically, this large savannah had been overlooked by private consultants contracted to devise a master management plan for the refuge. As a result, several water impoundments were under construction very near the savannah at the time of its rediscovery.

The intern reported the savannah to the staff at TNC's Midwest regional office, who consulted the book *Preserving Our Natural Heritage*, Volume I: *Federal Activities*,[5] to see what programs existed to protect areas owned by the U.S. Fish and Wildlife Service (FWS). The staff decided it would petition the FWS to designate the area as either a Research Natural Area or as a Public Use Natural Area.

On July 5, 1978, TNC and FWS officials—including the Sherburne refuge manager—met to discuss the designation proposal. FWS officials agreed that the savannah seemed to qualify as a Research Natural Area (RNA), but they wished to continue work on the water impoundments nearby. They decided to drill a series of test wells along a moisture gradient, allowing them to monitor any changes in the water table induced by flooding of land near the savannah.

On September 7, 1978, less than three months after the intern discovered an oak savannah at Sherburne, the Santiago Oak Savannah Research Natural Area was approved. In retrospect, several factors probably conspired to produce a speedy designation. One was the genuine enthusiasm of the FWS managers, particularly the Sherburne refuge manager. Another factor was the absence of a directly conflicting use of the land. The area was already a wildlife refuge. Once everyone agreed that designation would not interfere with construction of the impoundments, the RNA application gained momentum. Finally, the area was clearly and demonstrably important. Managers of public lands are generally eager— and are increasingly obligated—to know where such areas are located within their jurisdictions, to avoid damaging them, and to manage them so they will remain viable.[6]

Optimal Conditions for Designation

A public resource manager is most likely to agree to designate property under the following circumstances:

1. The area really is important.
2. Its importance—relative to any other parts of his domain—can be demonstrated clearly.
3. He has relatively little to lose in setting aside the area as opposed to using it in some other way.
4. Designation will not disrupt an existing program, particularly one regarded as important.
5. Designation helps the manager meet a legal obligation or a policy requirement.
6. Designation has popular support.

The two case studies above involved a collaboration of several agencies and individuals. In both instances the individuals who proposed the designation started from the bottom up. Rather than heading for Washington, they first enlisted the support of the people directly responsible for the day-to-day management of the land, then of the individual with direct control of the resource unit. A base commander, a forest supervisor or a refuge manager is as close to a sovereign as you will find. His support is essential.

Summary

Most public agencies established to manage natural resources have administrative programs that managers can use to set aside areas supporting elements of natural diversity. Some agencies require that lands set aside for conservation be formally withdrawn from uses permitted under conflicting laws. Lands designated by administrative rules enjoy no legal protection, but the protection can be strong if the relative significance of each designated area can be demonstrated clearly to policy makers and if designation helps fulfill a legal requirement, organizational incentive, or popular desire. Persons wishing to interest public officials in designating significant areas should compile a credible case and work locally at first.

APPENDIX A

The Nature Conservancy
BOARDMAN RESEARCH NATURAL AREA
Dedication & Field Trip

The Oregon Chapter

of

The Nature Conservancy

and the

Pacific Northwest Natural Area Committee.

Cordially Invite You

To The Dedication

of the

BOARDMAN RESEARCH NATURAL AREA

on

April 5, 1980 - 3:00 PM

at the

Boardman RNA - Boardman, Oregon

The trip will be highlighted by the dedication of the 5,000 acre Federal Research Natural Area with U.S. Navy officials, and observations of the nesting long-billed curlew, Swainson's hawks, ferruginous rough-legged hawks and burrowing owls.

This RNA, which is within the 46,000 acre Naval bombing range, is the finest remnant of native grassland remaining in the Columbia Basin. It also protects a highly visible section of the Old Oregon Trail.

SATURDAY, 5 APRIL

10:00 AM: Meet in Mayer State Park adjacent to the Conservancy's Rowena Dell Plateau Preserve where we will hike and enjoy the spring wildflower display. Take Old Columbia River Highway (US-30) from Mosier interchange on I-80N between Hood River and The Dalles to reach Mayer State Park. Bring a picnic lunch.

12:30 PM: Leave Rowena Dell.

2:00 PM: Meet at Boardman State Rest Stop located 22 miles east of Arlington on I-80N going east. From here we'll join our guide, Jeff Pampush and proceed in a caravan to the south end of the Boardman Bombing Range for the dedication. Turn off I-80N 4 miles east of Boardman on Heppner-Umatilla interchange and take road south (right) marked Heppner. This road parallels the east boundary of the bombing range and the caravan will turn in through gate 66 on the south end.

3:00 PM: Dedication of Boardman Research Natural Area, followed by birding and walk in Old Oregon Trail.

5:30 PM: Return to motels or campground in Boardman.

7:00 PM: No host dinner at Dodge City Inn/100 First NW/Boardman, Oregon.

SUNDAY, 6 APRIL

8:00 AM: Caravan leaves from Dodge City Inn parking lot for trip into north end of the Research Natural Area and returns at Noon. Those wishing to be out at daybreak on the grasslands when curlews are most active can meet at 5:30 AM and return for breakfast.

ACCOMMODATIONS: You should make your own advance reservations at one of the three Boardman motels or camp in the Boardman Marine Park on the Columbia River on the north edge of the town.

Dodge City Motel	481-2451
Nuggett Motel (Best Western)	481-2375
Riverview Motel	481-2775

Please call the Oregon Field Office of The Nature Conservancy if you plan to attend the field trip and advise the number that will be in your party. Phone: 228-9561.

Indiana Natural Areas Registry Brochure

79

CHAPTER EIGHT

MANAGEMENT AGREE-MENTS, LEASES, RIGHTS OF FIRST REFUSAL

So far the tools we've considered have been voluntary. Landowners noti-fied have not been asked to give up much of anything. Those who signed voluntary agreements could break them at any time. This chapter consid-ers three tools that up the ante a bit—though not much—giving us some control over the current use of a significant natural area or assigning us a privileged position in the marketplace.

These three tools—management agreements, leases, and rights of first refusal—provide a sort of middle ground for negotiating with landowners who will commit themselves to conservation practices but who will not permanently restrict the deed to their property. Each of these tools is a contract, meaning that each creates a legal interest in property that is granted in exchange for "consideration" (a nominal sum of our money usually) and that therefore can be recorded with the clerk of the county in which the property is located.

None of the three tools conveys a permanent interest in the areas we wish to protect—someone else still owns them—but, particularly if we can combine these tools on one property, we can control both the present and the future without (yet) having to spend much money.

This chapter will consider these concepts one at a time, then examine a case study for each.

Management Agreements

Management agreements are contracts between landowners and con-servationists, obligating the landowner to manage his property in a specific way for a stated period of time to achieve purposes mutually understood.

These agreements are well suited for private landowners who have tra-ditionally and consciously managed their property for natural values. Accordingly, management agreements are a commonly accepted way to protect natural areas in Great Britain, where personal stewardship of pri-vate land is a genteel tradition. In fact, nearly two-thirds of the nature reserves controlled by The Nature Conservancy of England are protected through management agreements.[1]

Even though the United States can claim no formal tradition of stewardship, there are stewards in this country as well. Many property owners have carefully protected the prairie remnants or virgin forests on their land, sometimes sacrificing income to do so. And yet the same emotional bond to land that inspires stewardship sometimes keeps owners from wanting to deed away rights. "I already take care of it," they are apt to say, pointing to a rookery or to a group of big trees as evidence, "why should I trust you to do any better?"

Many such landowners, in the course of their conservation efforts, have observed troubling or puzzling changes on their land and are not quite certain what to do about specific problems. A stand of giant trees begins to disintegrate, or cheatgrass invades an old patch of prairie, or a nesting pair of eagles stays away three years in a row. These owners usually welcome the chance to discuss these events and problems with an expert, and might enter into a carefully structured stewardship plan which involved professional monitoring and guidance. Owners who have cared enough to protect natural elements might appreciate the help of serious professionals who share their respect and concern. It is for these people that management agreements are ideal.

Terms and Enforcement. If the agreement involved consideration and has been legally recorded, it has given you an interest in the property. It is a valid contract and is theoretically enforceable throughout its duration, even though your stake in the property may be small. Many management agreements provide that the agreement can be broken anytime by either party, but that whoever wants out must first give the other 30 days' notice. The 30 days can give you time to try to rebuild the agreement or devise a new strategy. If the present owner intends to sell the property, a recorded agreement will crop up when the prospective buyer has the title searched. His attorney will almost certainly contact you to see if you believe you still have any interest in the property. At that time perhaps you can arrange to extend the agreement or discuss other protection ideas.

The agreement can be tailored to suit both parties, the more specific the management provisions, the better. Know clearly how you want the property to be managed, make it possible for the owner to do his part, and make sure you can monitor the arrangement.

Litigation should be a last resort, considered only if an injunction could prevent the owner from breaking the agreement in a way that would destroy something truly precious and irreplaceable. At best you could probably only postpone the action anyway, since his 30-day agreement termination notice would probably be right on the heels of your legal papers.

The agreement can endure as long as both parties desire. Agreements in Great Britain typically extend between 14 and 99 years, much longer than most agreements in the United States, which are characteristically renewed each year as long as both parties are content.

Leases

Leases describe rental agreements. You pay rent and take temporary possession of a property in order to control its use. The lease states the terms of the agreement, including what you (the lessee) may or may not do, what the property owner (lessor) retains, how long the lease will last, how much rent you pay, and how you pay it.

Usually, residential leases give you exclusive right of access to the property for a stated period of time, frequently one year. Thus you can control visitation, an important right when trying to protect something fragile or vulnerable.

The major distinctions between leases and the management agreements described earlier are probably more perceived than real, but they are important nonetheless. Corporations, public agencies, and individuals who own much land are familiar with leases since they have probably leased property to generate income from land assets. Conversely, management agreements connote a personal arrangement and are more closely associated with individual owners of private land, as in Great Britain. Leases tend to exist in standard form, tailored by amendments. Management agreements are more often crafted from scratch, even though they may be modeled after leases.

The lack of familiarity with management agreements can cause problems. A regional staff attorney for The Nature Conservancy has found that some county recorders will not record things called "management agreements," even though they convey the same interests in property as leases. To get these contracts recorded this attorney has instructed negotiators in his region to refer to all such arrangements as "lease and management agreements."[2]

Recording of leases is especially important. Many large firms lease thousands of tracts, and the modest rental agreement, which to you represents another plank in the ark, may mean something less to a corporation. It produces nominal rent, is something else to keep track of, and could get lost in the shuffle. Your landlord might inadvertently sell your leasehold without giving you 30 days' notice. When you next appear to inspect the premises, it may be posted and your interest destroyed. But a recorded lease should be noticed in a title search. If the property is sold, at least the new owner will have been notified that his activities are subject to your lease. It is probably easier to defend the terms of a lease than a recorded agreement since judges are particularly well acquainted with the instrument that has probably inspired more case law than any other.

Rights of First Refusal

Stated simply, a landowner can promise that if he ever decides to sell his property, he'll offer it to you first. Thus he gives you a superior position in the marketplace. The promise can be worth a lot, particularly if the owner will also agree to manage the property to protect the natural elements that concern you until he decides to dispose of it.

The "right of first refusal," or "first option to purchase," usually takes the following form: A landowner agrees, frequently for a small sum of money (the "consideration"), that if he ever receives a genuine offer for his property, he'll give you a certain period of time to match it before selling his property to anyone else.

There are a couple of potential catches. For one, you have to make sure he has received a genuine, bona fide offer. A scoundrel might try to invent an offer or persuade an accomplice to make an inflated offer in hopes of baiting you into matching it. Thus for your protection you must have the property appraised before exercising your option. Also, the period of time that a public agency has to match the offer (commonly 30 days) is sometimes too brief to arrange for an appraisal and come up with the money. Some states require an act of legislature and a specific appropriation for each purchase.

The 30-day match-time has become a self-defeating convention. New statutes and policy statements commonly tie the hands of agencies by giving them only 30 days to produce what is usually a hefty sum of money. There is no reason why an agency shouldn't negotiate for as much breathing room as possible, case by case. But even with more time, a public agency may have to try to extend the option, pay on an installment basis, or find a nonprofit ally, such as The Nature Conservancy, to prepurchase the property until acquisition funds become available.

Also, there is the issue of enforceability. What if you discover that the owner has rudely ignored your first option and sold his property to someone else? Rights of first refusal are interests in real property and should be recorded. To strengthen your legal claim, pay the landowner something, draw up a contract, and proceed to the county courthouse.

A right of first refusal is an option, not an obligation. You don't *have* to buy the property when it becomes available. Thus for a nominal fee you have purchased:

1. The right to know that the owner of an important tract is considering an action that could jeopardize the natural features you wish to protect.
2. Thirty days or so to negotiate with the owner before he can sell.
3. Usually, the ability to talk to the person who made the offer, to discern his attitude toward protection, and thus the ability to gauge how he would manage it if you let him go ahead and buy the property.
4. The ability to make an offer.

That's not bad for $10.

Several European countries have taken the concept a step further. So that municipalities could control enough land for municipal development, some agencies have been granted by law the "right of preemption." Theoretically, specified public agencies could buy up every piece of property whenever they appeared on the market by matching an offer within a certain period of time. Of course, the strength of the concept depends largely on how much money the agency has to acquire desirable properties.[3]

In this country, rights of first refusal are gaining currency as a way to protect natural areas. The innovative Mississippi Natural Heritage Act, described more fully in Chapter Twelve, provides that all Mississippi property owners who agree voluntarily to register their property must also grant the Mississippi Wildlife Heritage Committee first option to purchase the property should they decide to sell it. Missouri has also attempted to persuade registrants to grant the state a right of first refusal, although this is a matter of policy, not law, as it is in Mississippi.

Because Missouri's Department of Conservation hopes to someday acquire all areas registered voluntarily, department representatives seek first options to purchase whenever they ask landowners to sign voluntary protection agreements. Missouri's standard voluntary protection agreement contains a clause giving the state the right of first refusal. After clearly explaining the concept, Missouri negotiators leave it to the landowners to ask that the clause be removed.[4]

It may be that by legally requiring property owners who volunteer to register their property to also grant the state the right of first refusal, Mississippi has limited its ability to negotiate voluntary agreements. There may be a range of owners who would respond to a plaque or certificate but who would balk at any kind of legal agreement with the state. On the other hand, Mississippi's legislators may have endowed its land acquirers with a busy and rosy future, especially if they remember to give them some money. Time will tell.

Case Study:
The Ford Eagle Nesting Management Agreement

In June 1978 the director of The Nature Conservancy's Michigan field office received a call from a developer. The developer wished to know how much room you have to leave a nesting bald eagle in order not to disturb it. "Why?" replied the Michigan representative. It seemed the developer was about to bid on a parcel of lakefront property on Michigan's Upper Peninsula soon to be auctioned by the Ford Motor Company.

The field director quickly discovered that the tract in question contained a stand of white pine trees that harbored the last of four eagle nests at the lake, occupied intermittently since 1927 (one of the three other nests had been abandoned and two had been destroyed by residential development). Both the U.S. Forest Service and the State Department of Natural Resources knew about the Ford site and, in fact, knew that it currently contained an active nest with two eggs. They agreed that the eagles could not tolerate development of the tract.

The Conservancy's representative phoned the director of Ford's land division, who knew nothing of the nests. Although it was only ten days before the sealed bids were to be opened, Ford decided to postpone the sale until its executives had a clearer sense of whether the eagles could tolerate residential development of the tract.

Ford gave The Nature Conservancy $1,000 to develop an ecological inventory and management plan, which was completed in mid-November 1979. The plan mapped the nests, chronicled their nesting history, and proposed primary and secondary zones of protection around the nesting trees. The plan also recommended that Ford keep the property and allow TNC to manage it according to the terms of a written agreement.

The main provisions of the agreement include:

1. That Ford designate the property the "Ford Eagle Preserve."
2. The agreement be automatically renewable on an annual basis.
3. That the Conservancy pay Ford the consideration of $1 per year.
4. That the Conservancy supervise scientific, educational, and research activities on the property.
5. That Ford pay all taxes on the property.

The duration of the agreement is wisely linked to the tenure of the eagles at the site. The agreement would terminate if:

1. There are no viable nests on the property for five consecutive years.
2. Ford sold, leased, or otherwise disposed of the property.
3. Either party wanted out, on 60 days' notice.

Consideration ($1) would be granted and the agreement would be recorded. At this writing the agreement awaits final signatures. One factor in Ford's involvement has been the Conservancy's willingness and ability to publicize the agreement—and Ford's generosity—without revealing precisely where the nests can be found. This is not a cynical attitude on Ford's part. Its land managers are genuinely interested in protecting the eagles and deserve credit for their role in a collaborative effort. Indeed, the protection effort really began with Ford's decision to leave the bid envelopes sealed.

It works out well for the Conservancy, too, since they would prefer not to acquire this parcel as long as they feel confident Ford will protect it, since its sole ecological distinction is held irregularly in the boughs of a single white pine.

Case Study:
A Lease to Protect *Iliamna remota*

Iliamna remota (the Kankakee mallow) is a tall, showy, and extremely rare mallow whose pink blossom appears in late June. The species was discovered in 1878 by a Chicago University botanist who believed it to be unique to the Kankakee River island where he found it. He wasn't far from wrong; in the ensuing century only three more colonies have turned up.

The rarity of the species has brought it some renown. In 1920 Willard N. Clute, writing in the *American Botanist* called it "the rarest American plant." Fifty-five years later Dr. Earl Core, writing about a colony he discovered in 1927, allowed that crown to slip a little, calling it merely "the rarest Appalachian plant." At least three of the four known sites have been repeatedly visited and well studied. One colony is protected within an Illinois State Nature Preserve.

One group of the mallows sprouts alongside a railroad track in southern Virginia. Most of the plants are well within the 18-foot right-of-way that extends from the center line of an active freight line. The tracks are owned by the Chessie System, a large Cleveland-based corporation that counts three railroads among its assets. Somehow the plants have escaped (or perhaps thrived upon), the regimen of burning, spraying, and uprooting performed annually along all Virginia railroad tracks.

The existence of the trackside colony was brought to the attention of the mid-Atlantic field office of The Nature Conservancy by a member of the staff of the West Virginia Heritage Program. As of this writing, Virginia does not have a heritage program, but the West Virginia heritage staff botanist knew that *Iliamna remota* was being studied as a potential endangered plant species in Virginia.

In February 1979 a Nature Conservancy staff member, hoping to protect the colony, called on the chief engineer of Chessie's Richmond, Virginia, field office. The engineer had never been told about the plants, but his interest was aroused. He and his assistant promptly set about trying to locate the site on a track section map. Many maps later they found it. Within a week, on a bitter February day, he met a Conservancy representative at the site where together they surveyed the colonies.

"Next," he said, "you'll have to deal with the real estate section. I don't know what they'll want to do, but they might lease it to you." He was right. At Chessie's regional headquarters in Baltimore, the director of the real estate department refused immediately to sell or donate the land within the 18-foot primary or 50-foot secondary track right-of-way. He cited as a reason the company's legal obligation to control the use of land within those corridors, particularly in an emergency.

He proposed that Chessie lease the land to the Conservancy on an annual basis. Railroad companies like leases, which give them both income and control. Chessie has issued thousands of leases along its track corridors for various purposes.

After several weeks of negotiations, which took place mainly by exchange of draft leases, a lease was signed, which—for an annual rent of $50—gave The Nature Conservancy the following rights:

1. To erect a fence around the plants.
2. To post signs on the fence instructing Chessie personnel not to cut, spray, or burn the plants within. Chessie pledged that their local personnel would cooperate.
3. In the words of the lease, "to remove the rare plants for transplanting to other than railway property, should it be decided, at a later date, that the premises are required for other purposes."
4. To receive 30 days' notice should Chessie decide to withdraw from the lease, and by extension, 30 days to figure out how best to protect the plants.

The lease is renewable annually. The Conservancy is able to encourage and control scientific study of the plants on the property. One immediate study topic will be to determine the biological requirements of *Iliamna remota* on the site and to locate a transplant site should an emergency ever arise.

The lease is not ideal from the Conservancy's standpoint. The Conservancy would have preferred a longer term and a clear statement that the railroad is liable for injuries to its employees sustained at the site. Still, Chessie demonstrated a commitment and a sense of responsibility to the mallows, and the Conservancy gained, for a rent that is almost nominal, the ability to protect perhaps "the rarest Appalachian plant."

Case Study:
Rights of First Refusal

One of the more challenging protection efforts The Nature Conservancy has attempted was described briefly in Chapter Four. It is the kind of multi-tract welter of partial interests in property that a real estate pro wouldn't wish on his worst enemy. But the system of freshwater, interdunal pools at stake is such an important component of North Carolina's ecological heritage that the Conservancy's state representative decided to take it on.

One thing he knew from the start: he didn't have enough money to buy even the critical core required to give some immediate protection to the forest, let alone to purchase any bufferage against future encroachments. Upon investigating the ownership of the 14 tracts of property involved, he noticed that one family (call them Smith)—descendents of the recipient of an original land grant—owned four of the most significant parcels. Interestingly, only two of these tracts, situated near the southern limit of the forest, were contiguous; the others were separated by parcels owned by nonfamily members. It was clear that the Smith family's attitude was crucial: its opposition could destroy the project, but its support could provide a base of support for dealing with a total of seven tracts.

The family included a husband and wife, two children, and an aunt, all of whom had a stake in at least one parcel. (For example, the aunt owned a one-third undivided interest in one parcel.) Happily, it turned out that all had heard of and respected The Nature Conservancy, and all were interested in protecting the forest, whose significance was apparent to them.

Still, different family members wanted to do different things with the properties they owned. The children desired some immediate income from the property, and all wanted to reserve at least an acre on someone's plot for a family dwelling. They invited the Conservancy's representative to propose a protection scheme for their properties.

The Conservancy's representative had some desires too. Mainly, he wanted to protect the whole forest as strongly as possible without plunging the North Carolina field office into eternal debt. There are three tracts in between the four owned by the Smith family. He knew that at least two of these three owners would negotiate with him only if some cash were involved. He also knew that if either of them heard that the Smiths were cooperating on all of their four parcels, each would assume (correctly) that he possessed an inholding for which the Conservancy could be expected to pay top dollar. That would make negotiating much tougher.

The Conservancy representative decided to move quietly and to create at least the local illusion that he was proceeding monolithically northward. He proposed to the Smith family that they grant to the Conservancy conservation easements on their two adjacent southern parcels, and also grant the right of first refusal to purchase the two other isolated northern tracts. He trusted the family's commitment enough to know that they would protect the northern properties until they were ready to dispose of them, at which time the Conservancy or a public agency might be better able to make an offer.

The family consented under two conditions. The parents owned one of the two tracts outright and had willed it to the children. They decided to transfer title immediately to the children, then the children in turn agreed to grant the Conservancy first option to purchase it should they ever want to sell it. Secondly, the family wished to exempt one acre, on a noncritical area, from the agreement, so that they could build a family cottage.

The Conservancy representative agreed. The papers were executed and recorded. For $20 the Conservancy had gained the following:

1. The protection of two critical parcels, since the family has demonstrated a united commitment to the overall protection of the forest.
2. The ability to spend its limited acquisition dollars on other parcels.
3. A strategic advantage, earned by operating in a way that did not alert potential inholders.
4. Most important, momentum for the entire project.

Summary

Management agreements, leases, and rights of first refusal offer a middle ground of protection between purely voluntary agreements and acquisition of significant rights in property. Management agreements, which are ideal in working with owners who already practice some form of stewardship, obligate a property owner to manage his property in a specific way for a stated period of time. Leases are rental agreements, distinctive from management agreements mainly in that they are well known and understood, both by property owners and by recording agents. Rights of first refusal protect natural elements by giving conservationists an advantage in the marketplace. All three tools convey interests in real property to conservationists and should be recorded.

CHAPTER NINE

ACQUISITION OF FEE TITLE

Property law professors like to compare owning a piece of property to owning a bundle of sticks: each stick corresponds to a right in property, such as the right to live on the property, to will it to a relative, or to cut the trees that grow on it. A person who owns all the rights over property that the law allows—the entire bundle of sticks—is said to own "fee title" to the property. Fee title is the largest estate that the law allows.

Each right can be separated from the others and sold, bartered, or traded on the open market as an "interest" in property. Each interest has as much value as someone will pay for it, or, rather, could be expected to pay for it in unpressured circumstances. If you own the fee title to a piece of property, you probably possess rights and interests you don't even know about. Someone may appear one day to inform you that from the road your hedgerow appears to be full of quail, and he may ask your permission to hunt them. You have the legal right to say yes or no and the option to try to sell your hunting right for a fee.

The only limits to your domain are legal limits. You possess no more rights than the law allows. You can give or sell the right to hunt quail, but you can't authorize someone to hunt out of season. That property owners are subject to a variety of laws, ordinances, and regulations is well known and something of a sore point at times.

This chapter will consider why every state natural diversity effort must include the ability to acquire property. We'll also look at federal tax incentives for donors of ecologically important areas, and at several of the many ways donations can be made, comparing the tax savings achieved by each method. The chapter will also examine how public agencies and private organizations can work together on acquisition projects, discuss several federal programs that offer grants to acquire natural areas, consider the contribution that corporations can make to a conservation program, and offer a series of ideas for conservationists to consider in negotiating with landowners.

How Acquisition Fits into a
Good State Natural Areas Program

Chapter Four considered why a program designed to protect the remainder of a state's ecological heritage cannot consist solely of a land acquisition effort. The decision to seek to acquire property must be balanced against other conservation options, first considering:

1. The ecological significance of the property tract.
2. Whether or not the natural features are now protected.
3. The owner's attitude toward his property.
4. The price and whether you have enough money to spend.
5. If you succeed, whether you really want to manage the property. If not, who will?

Still, a credible statewide protection program simply must include land acquisition dollars, and the more dollars the better. Because ownership of fee title provides fullest legal control over property, we must have some ability to purchase the property that is most significant and least protected, and some ability to react quickly when a coveted parcel suddenly appears on the market.

South Carolina offers a good example. In 1976 the state legislature passed a progressive and innovative law establishing a formal program to protect the state's natural areas and providing authority for several different protection techniques.[1] The same legislature has never appropriated capital funds earmarked to acquire natural areas. It is presently possible to obtain acquisition money in South Carolina only by asking the legislature to fund specific projects through the Recreation Land Trust Fund, administered by the South Carolina Department of Parks, Recreation, and Tourism. There is no budget for natural areas. As a result, not a penny of state money has been spent to acquire a natural area since 1974, a fact which all but nullifies an excellent natural areas statute.

By contrast, the Ohio general assembly has appropriated $1,872,000 since 1974, resulting in the acquisition of 1,600 acres of Ohio's natural heritage. Missouri has perhaps the most remarkable program of all. In a 1976 referendum Missouri citizens voted to amend the state constitution to impose upon themselves a general sales tax of 1/8 cent on every dollar in order to finance a program to conserve forestry, fish, and wildlife resources. In the first two years alone over $51 million has been spent to acquire about 78,000 acres in 75 counties. The promise to protect endangered species' habitats and natural areas figured into the popular appeal of the measure.

States have dreamed up all sorts of ways to finance conservation programs, such as cigarette taxes (Texas), real estate transfer taxes (Maryland), license fees (Mississippi), income tax check-offs (Colorado), excise taxes; user fees, bond issues, legislative appropriations—but it has taken will and initiative to bring these into being.[2]

This chapter will offer only a skeletal perspective on land acquisition. Because traditionally in this country natural resource conservation has meant land acquisition, detailed accounts, founded on a substantial body of case experience, have been published on how to acquire land. The best known and most instructive of these accounts was prepared in 1975 by two staff members of The Nature Conservancy to aid them in teaching certain land acquisition techniques to a group of real estate negotiators working for what was then the Bureau of Outdoor Recreation (now absorbed into the Heritage Conservation and Recreation Service, or HCRS).[3] HCRS has updated this material to reflect changes in federal tax laws, and it is contained in a publication entitled *Land Conservation and Preservation Techniques,*[4] available free by writing to HCRS Information Exchange, U.S. Department of the Interior, Heritage Conservation and Recreation Service, Washington, D.C. 20243.

The basic presentation below cannot begin to convey the potential for creativity in negotiating for fee title, potential made possible mainly by flexible tax laws. Skillful negotiators acquire property by improvising upon a few basic themes to match the infinitely variable needs and desires that landowners have.

Land Acquisition and Federal Taxes

Our federal government encourages charity. The federal tax laws, compiled in the Internal Revenue Code, allow corporations and individuals to deduct from taxable income the value of gifts donated to schools, churches, hospitals, social welfare organizations, and publicly supported charities, including most conservation organizations. This encouragement of charity, tracing back to a belief in the separation of church and state and cumulatively reinforced by the practical realization that society needs the services performed by charities, has enabled public agencies and private organizations to acquire land that would otherwise be unobtainable.

Conservation of natural resources has long been a major social goal in the United States. Scores of federal laws proclaim the importance of conserving wilderness or wild rivers or habitats for endangered species. For example, section (2)(a)(4) of the Endangered Species Act of 1973 states:

> The United States has pledged itself as a sovereign state in the international community to conserve to the extent practicable the various species of fish and wildlife and plants facing extinction.[5]

In discussing the deductibility of donations to charitable organizations, the Internal Revenue Code, under sections 501 and 170, sets out the various social causes that the government considers important enough to merit charitable tax incentives. In addition, the code regulates charitable organizations to which interests may be donated and dictates the circumstances under which deductions of gifts can be claimed.

While the code does not state specifically that land conservation is an eligible social cause, it does recognize public agencies and certain land conservation groups as organizations to which people or corporations may donate land, money, or other interests and apply for a charitable deduction. At section 170(f)(3)(C), the code also provides us with a definition of the term "conservation purposes," including:

> (i) the preservation of land areas for public, outdoor recreation or education, or scenic enjoyment;
> (ii) the preservation of historically important land areas or structures; or
> (iii) the protection of natural environmental systems.

The tax code's acknowledgment that gifts for conservation purposes are deductible, coupled with the favorable tax treatment given to land conservation organizations, indicates the federal government's commitment to land conservation.

Incentives for Donations

Federal tax laws allow an individual or corporation to deduct from taxable income the appraised value of a gift of land to a federal, state, or local agency or qualifying charitable organization up to—in the case of most individuals—30 percent of one's adjusted gross income. Furthermore, individuals are allowed to spread out the deduction over six years —the year of the gift and the next five years (a major incentive since a tract of property is frequently worth more than 30 percent of one's adjusted gross income).

There is another compelling incentive too. Anyone who sells "capital gains property" (such as land or stock held for 12 months or more) has to pay taxes on the profit, which is the difference between the original purchase price ("basis") and the selling price, minus costs such as brokers' commissions and legal fees. By giving the property, one can completely avoid a capital gains tax, a major factor if the property is worth a lot more now than when the owner acquired it.

This is a simple view of an extremely complicated picture. The tax laws are baroque in their complexity, and they change all the time. Anyone—agency, organization, or landowner—should have the aid of a good tax lawyer before testing these waters.

Ways of Giving

Following are brief descriptions of several ways landowners commonly give land to nonprofit organizations or public agencies in order to protect natural features and take advantage of federal tax incentives. "Fair market value," a term which will appear repeatedly, is commonly defined as the price at which a piece of land might be sold by a willing seller to a willing buyer, neither being under pressure to buy or sell and both having full knowledge of the facts. (In practice this definition proves quite hypothetical since the buyer or seller is almost always under some form of pressure, and one usually knows more than the other.)

An Outright Donation. The owner can give land to an agency or non-profit organization with no strings attached through a standard deed of conveyance. This is the simplest and most direct land gift and usually provides the greatest tax benefits to the donor.

The maximum income tax advantages of such a gift go to the donor who gives highly appreciated property (land worth much more now than when the owner acquired it), is in a high income bracket, and is able to deduct the entire market value of the property within a six-year period.

A Bargain Sale. A bargain sale is part sale and part gift of land; it is a sale of land at less than its fair market value. The seller can deduct as a charitable contribution for income tax purposes the difference between the fair market value of the property and the actual sales price.

The bargain sale concept is very popular—it seems to offer something for everyone. The seller receives some immediate income and can deduct the value of the gift portion from income taxes, although he usually has to pay taxes on the capital gain. The value of his deduction can keep him in a lower tax bracket. The receiver, of course, gets to protect a significant area at a reduced cost.

A Donation with a Reserved Life Estate. An individual can donate property to an organization but continue to own it and live on it until he dies. When he gives a residence or farm subject to a life estate, the donor can deduct the value of his gift, called a "remainder interest," as a charitable contribution at the time of the gift, even though the organization will not actually take control until he dies. The same rules apply to a gift of a natural area subject to a life estate, provided that the remainder interest is given exclusively for conservation purposes.

The value of the deduction is the present fair market value of the property reduced by the value of the retained interest, as determined by actuarial tables published by the Internal Revenue Service. For a young donor, the value of the gift will be very little compared to the full present fair market value of the property (a fastidious reader might voice the mild objection that discussion of this strategy does not belong in a chapter on fee title acquisition since the owner still retains at least one stick in the bundle—the right of residency until he dies).

Those experienced with this concept advise the uninitiated to be prepared for management problems. Sometimes landowners who have grown fond of their property over the years see no reason why they can't transfer the life estate to a favored relative, or else five years later the owner suddenly needs money and wishes to renegotiate.

Remember that the landowner can still do with his property all that his deed allows during his lifetime. He could conceivably take actions that would destroy the element of natural diversity you wish to protect. If there are precious and destructible features on the property, it will probably be necessary to protect them through separate agreements, such as conservation easements (see Chapter Ten), or through restrictions in the owner's deed.

Donation of Undivided Interest in Land. When an "undivided" interest in property is contributed, the donor can deduct the fair market value of the interest contributed. Here the donor gives a percentage of his total legal interest in the land, rather than any specific physical portion.

As a result, the land is owned commonly as a unit by all those parties who have an interest in the property. Theoretically, all such owners have equal rights to possession of the property (condominium owners are familiar with this concept).

There may be a number of advantages to a donation of an undivided interest. To avoid concentrating his tax liability, the owner may wish to apportion the gifts through a measured series of percentage donations, or he may simply wish to continue to be a common owner of the land for a while.

If the donor intends to string out gifts of undivided interest, he should describe the terms of the total transaction in his will so that his intentions will be honored even if he is not alive to oversee the entire transfer. Likewise, an organization receiving percentages of undivided interest over time would be wise to secure a lease for the remaining interest in the property so it can be managed as one unit.

Donations by Will. An individual can will land to an organization. A deduction from the value of one's gross (taxable) estate is allowed for property willed for public, charitable, or religious purposes. Unlike the charitable deductions allowed from taxable income, there are no percentage limitations or deductions from estate taxes (remember the 30 percent of adjusted gross income?).

The terms of the will may or may not restrict the use of the property, but whenever possible, the recipient should review the section of the will that applies to the land. If there is something wrong with the proposed bequest, it is easier to work it out with a living donor than an estate representative.

How the Major Acquisition Alternatives Work

Following is a situation created to illustrate and compare the tax effects of four methods of land acquisition—sale, bargain sale, outright donation, and reserved life estate.[6] Remember that it is the bottom line, or the net cost after taxes, of using each method that counts.

Scenario

Harmony Woods, a 60-acre parcel of land, is the most significant natural area in the town of Harmony, Transylvania. The property is owned by the three Dolt brothers (Larry, Curley, and Moe), the Good sisters, and the Harmony Grits Company in tracts of 10 acres to each. It was originally acquired some years ago at a cost of $50 per acre but now has a fair market value of $1,000 per acre.

Haphazard Development, Inc., has expressed an interest in buying all the land. The town of Harmony, however, wants to acquire the land for conservation purposes.

Each brother makes a salary of $35,000 a year, and each receives an additional $2,000 a year in interest from investments. They are all unmarried, and each has current itemized deductions of $4,000 a year.

Tax Results from an Outright Sale. Friendly Broker volunteered to approach Moe Dolt on behalf of the town of Harmony. Harmony would purchase the land at fair market value, provided of course that Friendly would receive a 10 percent commission. Moe seemed interested and asked Friendly to compute the tax consequences of the sale.

Results in terms of the year's spendable income are illustrated in Table 1.

Tax Results from a Donation. Moe's brother Curly Dolt decided to donate his 10 acres of Harmony Woods to the town of Harmony. He saw no problem in giving the land to the town free and clear. He requested only that a memorial be placed on the property in memory of his parents.

By donating the property, Curly would receive a $10,000 charitable contribution deduction and would avoid a 10 percent broker's commission. Results in terms of this year's spendable income may be illustrated in Table 2.

Tax Results from a Bargain Sale. Harmony officials decided to approach Larry Dolt and request a bargain sale. Penny Pincher, the brother's accountant, recommended a 50/50 split. In effect, Larry would be donating part of the property and selling part of the property. Larry acceded.

Like Curly, Larry avoided a 10 percent broker's commission by bargain selling the land. Results in terms of Larry's spendable income this year are illustrated in Table 3, and are compared to the options his brothers pursued.

Tax Results from a Life-Estate Transaction. Mrs. Betty Good is a 70-year-old widow. Her two married children have successful careers. She has a personal income of $37,000 a year and current itemized deductions of $4,000.

Mayor Doright has asked Betty if she would consider donating her land to the town. Although Betty was pleased that the town was interested in preserving her land, she didn't want to give up use of the property. Mayor

100

Table 1—Tax Results from an Outright Sale

	MOE'S INCOME WITHOUT SALE	MOE'S INCOME IF LAND SOLD
INCOME		
Salary and interest income	$37,000	$37,000
Plus: Capital gain	—	8,500
Gross income	$37,000	$45,500
Less: Capital gain deduction (60 percent)	—	(5,100)
Adjusted gross income	$37,000	$40,400
Less: Excess itemized deductions and exemptions*	(2,700)	(2,700)
Taxable income	$34,300	$37,700
TAXES		
Federal income tax (per tables)	$ 9,864	$11,530
State income tax (taxable income minus federal tax times 5 percent)	1,222	1,309
Total taxes	$11,086	$12,839
CASH RETURN		
Gross income	$37,000	$45,500
Plus: Basis	—	500
Less: Taxes	(11,086)	(12,839)
Net cash return after taxes	$25,914	$33,161

Note: State income taxes vary widely from state to state. For purposes of this example a 5 percent rate is used, applied to taxable income.

*To determine the amount of excess itemized deductions, apply this formula:

A.	Total itemized deduction	$4,000
B.	Minus the zero bracket amount (from appropriate tax table)	2,300
C.	Equals excess itemized deductions	$1,700
D.	Add in exemptions	1,000
E.	Total deductions for tax rate table taxable income	$2,700

Doright proposed an alternative. Mrs. Good could donate the property and retain a life estate. Thus, she could continue to live on the land and use it just as she had in the past. The donation would give her an immediate tax deduction equal to the value of the gift. The deduction would increase her spendable income.

Table 2—Tax Results from a Donation

	CURLY'S INCOME WITH DONATION	MOE'S INCOME WITH LAND SALE
INCOME		
Salary and interest income	$37,000	$37,000
Plus: Capital gain	—	8,500
Gross income	$37,000	$45,500
Less: Capital gain deduction (60 percent)	—	(5,100)
Adjusted gross income	$37,000	$40,400
Less: Itemized deductions	(12,700)	(2,700)
Taxable income	$24,300	$37,700
TAXES		
Federal income tax (per tables)	$5,679	$11,530
State income tax (taxable income minus federal tax times 5 percent)	931	1,309
Total taxes	$ 6,610	$12,839
CASH RETURN		
Gross income	$37,000	$45,500
Plus: Basis	—	500
Less: Taxes	(6,610)	(12,839)
Net cash return after taxes	$30,390	$33,161
Net cost of donation	$ 2,771	

By referring to the appropriate table in the Gift Tax Regulations, they determined that the present value of a remainder interest in property made by a 70-year-old single woman is 52.460 percent. (The percentage would be less if she were younger.) The value of her gift and the amount deductible is, therefore, $5,246 ($10,000 times .52460 remainder interest). Results in terms of the year's spendable income may be illustrated in Table 4.

Incentives for Corporations

The Internal Revenue Code also encourages corporations to donate property to public agencies and nonprofit organizations. Corporations can deduct the value of gifts of property worth up to 5 percent of the company's net income before taxes. Like individuals, corporations are able to

Table 3—Tax Results from a Bargain Sale

	LARRY'S INCOME WITH 50 PERCENT BARGAIN SALE	CURLY'S INCOME WITH DONATION	MOE'S INCOME WITH LAND SALE
INCOME			
Salary and interest income	$37,000	$37,000	$37,000
Plus: Capital gain	4,750	–	8,500
Gross income	$41,750	$37,000	$45,500
Less: Capital gain deduction (60 percent)	(2,850)	–	(5,100)
Adjusted gross income	$38,900	$37,000	$40,400
Less: Itemized deductions	(7,700)	(12,700)	(2,700)
Taxable income	$31,200	$24,300	$37,700
TAXES			
Federal income tax (per tables)	$ 8,490	$5,679	$11,530
State income tax (taxable income minus féderal tax times 5 percent)	1,136	931	1,309
Total taxes	$ 9,626	$ 6,610	$12,839
CASH RETURN			
Gross income	$41,750	$37,000	$45,500
Plus: Basis	250	–	500
Less: Taxes	(9,626)	(6,610)	(12,839)
Net cash return after taxes	$32,374	$30,390	$33,161
Net cost of donation	$ 787	$ 2,771	

spread the value of their donation over the five years following the gift. Thus, if a corporation could expect an income before taxes of $1 million annually for at least six years, it could write off the value of donated land worth $300,000 ($50,000, or 5 percent of $1 million, for six years).

Furthermore, by giving rather than selling property, corporations can avoid a tax rate of up to 46 percent on ordinary income, and a capital gains tax of up to 28 percent.

Your attempt to persuade a corporate executive to donate a natural area will be interesting. Because he is responsible ultimately to shareholders and is absorbed in an effort to turn a profit and attract new investors, the executive might not be overwhelmed by the elegance of your plan to protect the state's natural diversity.

Still, under certain conditions there are good reasons for the company to donate property:

1. The land may be remote, barren, wet, steep, or stubborn. Your island of diversity may be a corporation's dead asset. The company can reinvest tax savings into more profitable operations.
2. The company may have acquired these barren acres years ago for a song, and the property value may have appreciated dramatically. The capital gains savings could be tremendous.
3. The cost of carrying unproductive land may be gnawing at the company's margin. A well-structured proposal may be attractive if property taxes, liability insurance, and operation costs are becoming burdensome.
4. The gift of a significant natural area can generate very favorable publicity.

The Land and Water Conservation Fund

As noted earlier, The Land and Water Conservation Fund (LWCF), administered by the Heritage Conservation and Recreation Service (HCRS), is the prominent source of funds that public agencies use to acquire properties of natural, recreational, or historical significance. Sixty percent of the total fund, or about $300 million in the fiscal year 1980 budget, is available to state and local agencies, allocated mainly according to statewide population (so that in 1980 California got the most and Nevada the least).

The LWCF program is structured so that the federal government, through HCRS, will fund up to 50 percent of the fair market value of any land acquired by a public agency, if there is enough money in the fund and if the acquisition project has the support of the state HCRS liaison officer and the LWCF grant administrator within each state (see Key Contacts for a list of the state liaison officers).

104

Table 4—Tax Results from a Life-Estate Transaction

	INCOME WITHOUT DONATION	INCOME WITH DONATION
INCOME		
Adjusted gross income	$37,000	$37,000
Less: Excess itemized deductions and exemptions	(3,700)	(8,946)
Taxable income	$33,300	$28,054
TAXES		
Federal income tax (per tables)	$ 9,414	$ 7,143
State income tax (taxable income minus federal tax times 5 percent)	1,194	1,046
Total taxes	$10,608	$ 8,189
CASH RETURN		
Gross income	$37,000	$37,000
Less: Taxes	(10,608)	(8,189)
Net cash return after taxes	$26,392	$28,811
Value of gift to Betty		$ 2,419

Under ideal circumstances, which happen rather frequently, federal tax laws and HCRS policy can mesh so that a state or local agency can acquire property without paying a cent. For instance, a property owner could donate half the value of his property through a 50-percent bargain sale to, say, a state department of natural resources and write off the value of the gift. The agency could then use LWCF money to pay the remaining 50-percent sale price. Thus, the state would not have paid at all.

When the value of a gift to an agency has exceeded 50 percent of the fair market value of the property, HCRS has characteristically allowed the agency to "credit" the excess value to a future transaction. Suppose, for instance, that a landowner sold property appraised at $100,000 to the Transylvania Department of Natural Resources for only $30,000. In effect, the owner would have given the agency $70,000. HCRS would not fund more than 50 percent of the fair market value of the gift, but it might well allow the agency to apply now for $50,000 in matching funds and to credit the excess $20,000 of gift value for a future project. Volunteer services, materials, and equipment can also be used to match federal funds if HCRS wants what you have to offer. All in all, it is a remarkable arrangement.

Generally, for real property donated to a state or local agency to qualify as the nonfederal matching share of an LWCF project, the following criteria must be met:

1. The property must be made available for public outdoor recreation use (which can include "passive" activities such as hiking or nature study).
2. There should be no reversionary clause in the deed of conveyance.
3. An appraisal of the property must be approved by the Heritage Conservation and Recreation Service prior to the donation.
4. The land donation must not be accepted prior to HCRS project approval or a grant of waiver of retroactivity.
5. The transaction must honor appropriate local, state, and federal regulations.

Other Federal Programs

Even though the Land and Water Conservation Fund is the largest and best-known source of federal matching funds for acquisition of natural areas, there are many other programs with land acquisition budgets that can be used to purchase land when your objectives coincide with Congress's reason for appropriating the money (see Table 5).

Nonprofit Charitable Organizations

A serious statewide ecological protection program will need the help of private, nonprofit conservation organizations. The work of major, national groups such as The Nature Conservancy (whose primary objective is the preservation of natural ecological diversity) can be complemented by the establishment of local land trusts or conservation foundations.

Governmental agencies simply cannot carry the load alone. Many states do not yet have a natural area protection program as such, and at this writing half the states are without an integrated body of mapped ecological data which can pinpoint areas in greatest need of protection.

Federal conservation efforts are spread out over several agencies, effective in spots, but likewise without a focusing body of locational data. Furthermore, many landowners distrust government in any form and give

Table 5

**Some Federal Programs Which
Offer Matchable Grants for Land Acquisition**

Program	Administrative Agency	Statutory Authority	Grants Awarded	Percent (Fed/ Matched Loc)	Granting Scope
Historic Preservation Grants-in-aid	Heritage Conservation and Recreation Service	1935 Historic Sites Act	$17.5 million (1977)	50/50	Land with archaeological, cultural, or historic significance
Pittman-Robertson Grants	U.S. Fish and Wildlife Service, Office of Federal Aid	Federal Aid in Wildlife Restoration Act	$9.8 million (1978)	75/25	Feeding, nesting, or breeding places for wildlife
Dingle-Johnson Grants	U.S. Fish and Wildlife Service, Office of Federal Aid	Federal Aid in Fish Restoration Act	$2.1 million (1978)	75/25	Restoration and management of fish species of sport or recreational value
Endangered Species Habitat Acquisition*	U.S. Fish and Wildlife Service, Office of Endangered Species	1973 Endangered Species Act	$3.8 million (1978)	66⅔**/33⅓	To acquire habitat for listed endangered or threatened species
Resource Conservation and Development Grants	U.S. Soil Conservation Service	1962 Food and Agriculture Act	$6 million (1979)	Up to 50	Technical and financial assistance to local gov'ts in rural areas

*Some funds have been granted for species on statewide endangered species lists.
**U.S. Fish and Wildlife Service will put up 75 percent on approved projects covering two or more states with approved endangered species conservation plans.

107

negotiators representing public agencies a cold shoulder. And as discussed above, land acquisition funds are the trophies appropriated to winners of interdepartmental competitions. The traditional victors have been fish and game departments and parks agencies. Even for the winners, the money is not always available at the moment it is needed.

By comparison, private organizations can act more quickly and flexibly, and their representatives are sometimes welcomed or tolerated simply because they don't work for a public agency. Also, successful private groups are able to acquire areas that do not attract the interest of public agencies.

The work of The Nature Conservancy is cited throughout this volume. Through skillful use of tax incentives and careful planning, the Conservancy has assembled a system of over 680 preserves, comprising about 1.5 million acres. Many of these preserves were acquired cooperatively with public agencies. Less well known are the land trusts, concentrated mainly in New England, which have helped protect important areas known locally. Such groups have not yet concentrated on protecting elements of natural diversity that have been indicated by a statewide body of data, but in some instances they could do so.

The tax status assigned a land trust by the Internal Revenue Service is crucial to the group's ability to help donors receive the most beneficial tax treatment. The IRS cares mainly that the organization is indeed supported by a broad "public" constituency (and is not the brainchild of a small group of individuals seeking a tax shelter), and that land acquired be available to the public. The IRS is also concerned that the group have a clear sense of public purpose (again, the service desires to be convinced that a small group of individuals has not formed a trust in order to shelter land transactions among their peer group).

Anyone seriously interested in exploring conservation foundations as a way to protect significant elements of natural diversity should obtain IRS Publication No. 557 entitled "How to Apply for and Retain Exempt Status for Your Organization."

Remember that it is not always possible to protect natural areas by using a tool designed to stimulate public recreation. If you form a land trust, think carefully about the extent and impact of likely forms of recreation on fragile ecological areas.

As of this writing, 42 of the 50 states have exempted from property taxation land held and used for public purposes by charitable, nonprofit organizations. The exemption rewards the efforts of such groups to provide new public recreational opportunities, including "passive" opportunities for recreation such as hiking or birdwatching.

Negotiating Tips

You must be able to deal skillfully with landowners to use any of the tools described in this book. You'll have to convince most landowners that your idea satisfies his needs, that is, your perception of his needs. All of the tools offer financial and emotional incentives that must be presented clearly and compellingly. Here are a few tips:

1. Know what you want before you knock on the door.
2. Do your homework. Before you begin negotiating, check out all the facts, angles, and contingencies such as the ownership pattern, cost of the land, zoning, comparable values, real estate trends, owners' income brackets, family makeup, earning potential, attitudes, and affiliations. Have your case well prepared and to the point. Some negotiators prepare tax tables, keyed to several different income brackets and to an estimated value of a property before they meet the landowner. Thus, when negotiating, they are able to quickly demonstrate the rough consequences of several options without risk of insulting the owner by wrongly guessing his tax bracket (see Appendix A for an example of the tables).
3. Try to figure out what the other person wants and really needs.
4. Never be intimidated by somebody else's position. Successful people are usually very candid in their approach. Stand your ground.
5. Listen to what the other person is saying and respond accordingly.
6. Don't hesitate to inflate your opposite number, but stick to your point. Do not get sidetracked into meaningless conversation.
7. Negotiating is basically the art of compromise. A concession is worth what the recipient thinks it is worth, so make it worth everything you can get. Leave plenty of time. Do not let a plane schedule force you into a bad decision. Develop a strategy so that everyone wins on something.
8. Don't give in easily when asked to make concessions. Have some points that you can surrender, but remember that every concession must be worth something.
9. Use the tactic of limited authority where appropriate. Have a supe-

109

rior in the background with whom you must check when you reach a difficult situation.

10. Never get deadlocked. If you cannot reach an agreement on one point, set it aside and move on to another.

Summary

Acquisition of fee title entitles the owner to all rights in property the law allows. State protection programs must have some ability to purchase key properties and can obtain funding in many ways. Federal tax laws encourage landowners—including corporations—to donate property to public agencies or qualifying nonprofit conservation organizations. The Land and Water Conservation Fund is structured to assist public agencies acquire land for recreational purposes. Nonprofit organizations are characteristically able to acquire property quickly and flexibly and have frequently cooperated with public agencies in conservation efforts.

APPENDIX A
Open Sale: At Fair Market Value

If sales price is:	$100,000	$130,000
Basis	2,000	2,000
Capital gain	98,000	128,000
Federal tax gain at 40% of gain	39,200	51,200
State tax at 7%	6,860	8,960
Federal tax at:		
70%	$ 27,440	$ 35,840
60%	23,500	30,720
50%	19,600	25,600
NET after tax	(Sales price less state & federal tax)	
at 70%	$ 65,700	$ 87,300
60%	69,640	92,420
50%	73,540	97,540

100% Gift of Property

Assuming appraisal of $100,000	Tax savings
at 70%	70,000 + 2,100 = $72,100
60%	60,000 + 1,050 = 61,050
50%	39,600 + 525 = 40,125

Assuming appraisal of $130,000	Tax savings
at 70%	91,000 + 2,100 = $93,100
60%	78,000 + 1,050 = 79,050
50%	39,600 + 525 = 40,125

Bargain Sale I: 50% Bargain Sale

Assuming appraisal of:	$100,000	$130,000
SALE: 50% fair market value	$ 50,000	$ 65,000
Less ½ adjusted basis	1,000	1,000
Capital gain	$ 49,000	$ 64,000
Federal taxable gain at 40%	19,600	25,600
State tax at 7%	3,430	4,480
Federal tax at:		
70%	$ 13,720	$ 17,920
60%	11,760	15,360
50%	9,800	12,800

NET after tax

at 70%	$ 32,850	$ 47,080
60%	34,810	49,640
50%	36,770	52,200

VALUE OF GIFT:	$ 50,000	$ 65,000

Federal tax saving

at 70%	$ 35,000	$ 45,500
60%	30,000	39,000
50%	25,000	32,500

State tax saving

at 70%	$ 2,100	$ 2,100
60%	1,050	1,050
50%	525	525

NET return	Cash in hand + tax saving =	Cash in hand + tax saving =
at 70%	32,850 + 37,100 = $69,950	47,080 + 47,600 = $94,680
60%	34,810 + 31,500 = 66,310	49,640 + 40,050 = 89,690
50%	36,770 + 26,025 = 62,795	52,200 + 33,025 = 85,225

Bargain Sale II: 65% Sale/35% Gift

Assuming fair market value appraisal:	$100,000	$130,000

SALE: 65% fair market value	$ 65,000	$ 84,500
Less ⅔ adjusted basis	1,400	1,400
Capital gain	$ 63,600	$ 83,100

Federal taxable gain at 40%	25,440	33,240
State tax at 7%	4,452	5,817

Federal tax at:

70%	$ 17,808	$ 23,268
60%	15,264	19,944
50%	12,720	16,620

NET after tax

at 70%	$ 42,740	$ 55,415
60%	45,284	58,739
50%	47,758	62,063

VALUE OF GIFT:	$ 35,000	$ 45,500

Federal tax saving

at 70%	$ 24,500	$ 31,850
60%	21,000	27,300
50%	17,500	22,750

State tax saving		
at 70%	$ 2,100	$ 2,100
60%	1,050	1,050
50%	525	525

NET return	Cash in hand + tax saving =	Cash in hand + tax saving =
at 70%	42,740 + 26,600 = $69,340	55,415 + 33,950 = $89,365
60%	45,284 + 22,050 = 67,334	58,739 + 28,350 = 87,089
50%	47,758 + 18,025 = 65,783	62,063 + 23,300 = 85,363

Bargain Sale III: 65% Gift/35% Sale

Assuming fair market value appraisal:	$100,000	$130,000

SALE: 35% fair market value	$ 35,000	$ 45,500
Less ⅓ adjusted basis	700	700
Capital gain	$ 34,300	$ 44,800

Federal taxable gain at 40%	13,720	17,920
State tax at 7%	2,401	3,136

Federal tax at:		
70%	$ 9,604	$ 12,544
60%	8,232	10,752
50%	6,860	8,960

NET after tax		
at 70%	$ 22,995	$ 29,820
60%	24,367	31,612
50%	25,739	33,404

VALUE OF GIFT:	$ 65,000	$ 85,200

Federal tax saving		
at 70%	$ 45,500	$ 59,640
60%	39,000	51,120
50%	32,500	42,600

State tax saving		
at 70%	$ 2,100	$ 2,100
60%	1,050	1,050
50%	525	525

NET return	Cash in hand + tax saving =	Cash in hand + tax saving =
at 70%	22,995 + 47,600 = $70,595	29,820 + 61,740 = $91,560
60%	24,367 + 40,050 = 64,417	31,612 + 52,170 = 83,782
50%	25,739 + 33,025 = 58,764	33,404 + 43,125 = 76,529

CONSERVATION EASEMENTS

Conservation easements are restrictions that owners place on their property and that legally bind present and future owners. In other words, by granting a conservation easement over his property, the owner of fee title surrenders some—but not all—of the sticks in the bundle, transferring certain property rights to a party who has conservation in mind, usually a conservation organization or governmental agency. Thus, a person or group that has acquired a conservation easement is said to have acquired a "less-than-fee" interest property. By acquiring an easement, a conservation group is able to protect elements of natural diversity by controlling only the rights that an owner could use to destroy or degrade them. The group does not have to own, manage, or pay for the remaining rights or interests.

The terms of the arrangement, which are described in a legal document also called an easement (see Appendix A) can vary widely. They are tailored to match the desires of both the owner and the conservationist. Some allow limited structural development, hunting, farming, or grazing, while others provide that property must be left entirely in a natural condition. Many easements allow the landowner to reside on the property. Commonly restricted activities—which are not always utterly prohibited—include industrial development, subdivision, clearcutting, landscape alteration, erection of billboards, mineral development, or garbage dumping.

This chapter will discuss the different kinds of easements and will consider and evaluate the problems that public agencies have experienced in trying to use easements to control major resources. We'll look at state easement laws, income and property tax incentives to donors of easements, and the problems appraisers and assessors encounter in trying to evaluate partial interests in property. Finally, the chapter will consider the challenge of enforcing restrictions imposed "in perpetuity."

Classification of Easements

Strictly speaking, we have just defined a negative easement granted in perpetuity, meaning an easement that restricts forever the use of certain rights in a property. By contrast, rather than restricting himself, a property owner might grant rights such as hunting rights or the right to periodically burn a prairie to someone else through an easement, which would then be characterized as an affirmative easement.

These distinctions are part of a system of classifying easements that we have inherited from Roman law, that have been subsequently complicated by British law, and even further confused by American jurists. Major kinds of easements include:

Easements Appurtenant. Easements that "benefit" a contiguous (or appurtenant) property. For instance, suppose you convince your neighbor to grant you an easement allowing you to cross his property to reach a trout stream whenever you desire. The easement would be "appurtenant" because your properties adjoin and because the easement benefits one of the estates, namely yours. The benefited property is called the "dominant" estate and the "burdened" property (your neighbor's) is called the "servient" estate.

There is also a fairly sizable history of easements that are "visually contiguous," that is affecting properties not physically adjoining but within sight of each other. Several islands in Maine, for example, are protected through appurtenant easements, which are visually contiguous (except on foggy days).

Easements in Gross. An easement in gross belongs to its owner, regardless of whether or not he owns benefited property adjacent to the burdened estate. An easement granted by a Montana rancher to The Nature Conservancy, whose corporate offices are in Arlington, Virginia, is a good example of an easement in gross.

Term Easements. Easements that last for a specified period of time.

Easements in Perpetuity. Easements that last forever, "running with the land" and affecting everyone who will ever own the property.

Can Easements Be "Assigned"?

For nearly two centuries now, both American and British courts have debated the "assignability"[1] of easements, that is, whether easements can be bought, sold, inherited, donated, or swapped from owner to owner or whether they are instead personal arrangements between specific parties. This issue is very important if we are to use easements as a way to protect

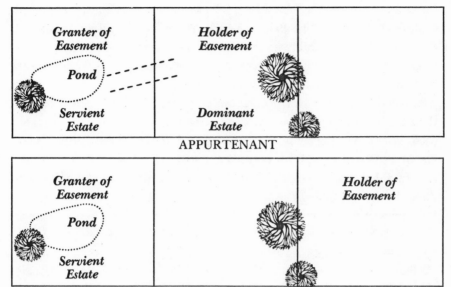

Comparison of an easement appurtenant and an easement in gross. A property that benefits from an appurtenant easement (the dominant estate) must adjoin—or at least be within sight of—the burdened (servient) estate. An easement in gross does not benefit an adjacent property, or in fact a property at all. Instead, it benefits a holder, which can be a conservation group seeking to protect the natural character of the servient estate.

natural features permanently, because terms will have to bind everyone who will ever own the property, and we will have to be able to enforce legally the terms of the easements if they are violated.

Before the nineteenth century, British common law courts favored easements appurtenant over easements in gross because benefits of tangible relationships were easy to understand in a simple, rural society. Jurists freely assigned the rights to graze, plant, plow, fish, or hunt on the other side of a fence from owner to owner of the dominant estate. Easements in gross appeared as Britain's post-industrial economy diversified and industrialists found the common law too rigid for the modern arrangements they sought.

By the turn of the nineteenth century British courts had adopted the view that persists in Britain today, allowing the creation of easements in gross only if the easement allowed the holder to make a profit, such as the right to enter a servient estate to mine coal. American jurisprudence, by fortunate contrast, has never made up its mind on the assignability of easements in gross. Like British judges, Americans regularly permitted the creation of profitable easements in gross, but beyond this point a broad diversity of decisions has developed, varying greatly from state to state, with no national consensus ever achieved. Today, 40 states have passed laws dealing with the creation, transfer, and enforcement of less-than-fee interests for conservation or preservation purposes. In 22 states these laws provide specifically that recorded conservation easements (or any of a spate of synonymous terms) can be assigned whether or not they benefit a dominant estate. Three other state statutes are only slightly less direct in accomplishing the same result (see Table 1).

Table 1—States with Laws Providing for Conservation Easements in Gross

*Arkansas	Illinois	Minnesota	*South Carolina
California	Indiana	*Montana	South Dakota
*Colorado	*Louisiana	*New Hampshire	*Utah
*Connecticut	Maine	New York	*Vermont
*Delaware	Maryland	*North Carolina	
*Florida	*Massachusetts	*Ohio	
*Georgia	Michigan	*Rhode Island	

*These statutes specifically authorize at least certain charitable nonprofit organizations to hold easements.

The trend is encouraging. Most of these 25 state laws have been passed since 1975, and 16 of them specifically authorize nonprofit, charitable organizations to hold easements. Most of these statutes specifically include within the scope of their authority the conservation of natural resources.

Because conservation easements offer a way for conservation agencies and organizations to acquire and control development rights without having to acquire the entire fee title, every state should have a good conservation easement law (a model conservation easement law appears as Appendix B). The statute should be drafted clearly, providing at least the following:

1. That easements in gross may be assigned.
2. That nonprofit, charitable organizations organized for conservation purposes should be allowed to hold easements.
3. That perpetual easements be allowed.
4. That in assessing property burdened by an easement for property

tax purposes, county or municipal assessors should reduce the assessment by the value of rights granted away.

Without such a law conservation groups usually must negotiate for easements appurtenant in order to protect natural features through easements. This complicates the task enormously because it forces the group to *own* a tract at least within sight of the target parcel. Usually that means asking the property owner to give or sell an acre or so to the conservation organization. Sometimes the owner is willing to grant an easement primarily because he doesn't wish to give or sell any of his property in fee. The problems are obvious.

Use of Easements in the United States by Public Agencies

Public agencies have used easements sporadically for over 50 years, frequently to control the rights to develop river or highway corridors, as shown in Table 2.

The efforts have tended to be massive and monolithic attempts to purchase easements from hundreds of owners at a "going rate," rather than specific attempts to control selected rights to significant properties. Most of these programs can claim at least partial success in achieving the protection desired, but the experience has nonetheless soured many federal officials on conservation easements. The Blue Ridge Parkway experience provides a case in point.

During the 1930s, the National Park Service (NPS) began to build scenic parkways through large wilderness areas, including the Blue Ridge Parkway, extending 47 miles through Virginia and North Carolina. To save money, NPS decided to purchase easements along highway corridors whenever possible, rather than acquiring fee title. It was arranged that Virginia and North Carolina state agents, presumably more credible to local landowners than NPS representatives, would negotiate the easements, then allow NPS to enforce their restrictions.

This apparently confused landowners and frustrated both state and federal officials, as the following account demonstrates.

The state agent had to concern himself only with getting the landowner's signature on the conveyance. The National Park Service received the full blame when it tried to explain to a bewildered farmer that he had sold some of his rights although he still "owned" his property and still held the deed to it. The lack of clarity of understanding was compounded when a second generation of owners came

119

Table 2—Selected Major Public Programs
Involving Purchase of Scenic or Conservation Easements[2]

PROGRAM AND AGENCY/STATE	WHEN ACQUIRED	ACRES
Blue Ridge Parkway, U.S. Park Service	1930s and 1940s	1,200
Natchez Trace Parkway, U.S. Park Service	1930s	5,000
Adirondack Northway Interchanges, New York	1960s	1,000
Piscataway, U.S. Park Service	1960s	2,000
Sawtooth National Recreation Area, U.S. Forest Service	1970s	10,000+
Wild and Scenic Rivers, U.S. Forest Service	1970s	5,000+
Waterfowl Management, U.S. Fish and Wildlife Service	1958-1977	1,100,000
Great River Road and other state highways, Wisconsin	1950s	17,000

along; that is, the sons or successors who had not signed the agreement and did not feel bound by it, even if they knew about it. This was soon followed by skyrocketing costs of patrolling because of the distance over which the easements extended and because the number of violations was steadily and substantially increasing.

In addition there were no set standards for the appraisal of the rights taken. The states were given a lump sum and instructed to buy as many easements as possible with it. As a result, there was a large amount of "dickering" and very little uniformity. When one farmer found out that he was paid only half what his neighbor received for the same easement, on like land, he was bitter. This in turn further encouraged violation of the agreement by the abused landowner.[3]

Confronted with mounting local hostility, NPS stopped at 177 easements in 1936. The agency has since spent over $5 million to purchase land in fee within the corridor.

In the early 1960s the state of Wisconsin likewise decided to use conservation easements in a big way. In 1961 Governor Gaylord Nelson thus exhorted the Wisconsin legislature:

> I propose that we use easements on a far broader scale, with a prospect of equal or even greater savings. In addition to scenic easements (along highways), I propose that we purchase public access rights, public hunting and fishing rights, use and alteration rights of headwaters and springheads, wetlands drainage rights, scenic overlook rights, fencerow rights for the protection of game cover, platting rights along trout streams, subdivision and timber cutting rights along lake shorelines, and development rights to protect lands adjacent to state parks and campgrounds from the clutter of billboards, taverns and concessions . . . In the ten year program, I propose that about $7.5 million of the $50 million total be reserved for these easements . . . Of the total acreage to be put under public control, more than one-third will be covered solely by easement rights.[4]

The legislators responded enthusiastically, approving Governor Nelson's proposals. A 1963 account shows the easement program ahead of schedule,[5] but by 1965 the bloom had started to fade. A 1974 account is an autopsy of a good idea that never fulfilled its youthful promise.[6] Only a tenth of Governor Nelson's $7.5 million had been spent on easements. Only 8.5 percent of all land protected was controlled through easements, as opposed to the one-third Governor Nelson had envisioned.

The reasons cited for the discouraging performance are similar to the Blue Ridge Parkway experience: Easements confuse landowners; easements confuse negotiators; they are hard to appraise, and are distrusted by local assessors.

These accounts and others suggest that the problem experienced may not rest entirely with the nature of easements, but also with the expectations people have for them and the scale with which they have been used. Agencies have tended to use easements faddishly, promoting them from time to time as the way to control a major area, becoming discouraged after awhile and then scrapping the whole idea. Out of favor, easements lie around for a time, gathering dust on the floor of a closet full of planning tools, only to be rediscovered periodically, picked up, and used again.

Efforts to apply one tool indiscriminately to protect vast areas with hundreds of property owners are almost bound to falter (even though the record is by no means one of uniform failure). There are certainly problems inherent in negotiating easements, but they could probably be mini-

121

mized if easements could be used as one of a series of negotiating options rather than as the centerpiece of a "program." Negotiators could probably begin to do better if:

1. They were not bound to negotiate for easements.
2. They clearly understood and were able to present income and capital gains tax advantages to donors of easements. It is not necessary always to purchase easements. (The Nature Conservancy has purchased only 1 out of more than 80.)
3. Before meeting a landowner, they had a clear idea of what rights were desired and not desired, and a good idea of the value of the rights to be obtained.
4. Negotiators offering to purchase easements could clearly explain all the factors considered to arrive at the proposed purchase price.
5. They were experienced, well-informed people who understood and believed in the protection objective.

How Much Are Conservation Easements Worth?

Tax assessors and conservationists have had a tough time trying to figure out how much conservation easements are worth. It would seem logical to consider the separate value of each right surrendered, total them up, and come up with a figure, but it's usually not so easy when you're working with an actual parcel of land.

Basically, the value of an easement compared to the fair market value of the entire fee title to a property depends upon:

1. The nature of the restrictions on development imposed by the easement.
2. How developable the property is without the restrictions.

Presumably, an easement granted that would prohibit structural development and cutting of timber on a rocky Maine seacoast, where soils are too shallow to percolate sewage or to produce many board feet of timber, wouldn't be worth much. On the other hand, an easement prohibiting tillage of black loam soil in Iowa in order to protect a prairie remnant might be worth as much as the entire fee.

Some agency officials have claimed that it makes more sense to negotiate for fee title, since they contend easements cost almost as much as fee title anyway, convey fewer rights, and are trickier to negotiate. Such observers doubt that the price of an easement really can reflect the actual value of rights surrendered relative to the value of all rights in a property. At least some experience seems to show otherwise.

The extent to which the marketplace can reflect the value of easements was tested in 1978 by two South Dakota economists who examined 134 transactions of northern prairie wetlands burdened by easements restricting drainage, burning, or filling (part of a U.S. Fish and Wildlife effort to protect glacially created "potholes" used by breeding waterfowl, which since 1958 has netted over 17,000 easements).[7] The economists assumed the value of a wetlands easement to be the net earnings the owner could have expected had he drained and filled the wetland, minus the cost of doing so.

The market proved very sensitive to wetland types (whether or not they were permanently flooded) and to their prevalent land use (cropland or grassland). Where drainage could increase agricultural output per acre dramatically, and it was not too expensive to drain the land, easements cost an average of about 60 percent of the whole fee. Where it just wasn't worth it to drain anyway, easements were all but free.

Their work shows that it is possible, by carefully considering potential earnings and enjoyment of rights to be forsaken, to calculate the value of an easement. But this doesn't mean it will happen. Tax assessors traditionally have been sluggish in granting reduced rates, and appraisers— who have a hard enough time trying to evaluate the *total* value of a property—sometimes view easements nervously. (There is a Wisconsin record of an appraiser who charged the state $8,000 to determine that an easement was worth $12,000.) As the many new state conservation laws generate new easements, standard regional appraisal practices keyed to land type, land use, and local economic conditions probably will evolve.

Tax Incentives to Donate Conservation Easements

The same basic rules governing donations of fee-simple interests in property that were described in Chapter Nine, apply to donations of conservation easements. You can even make a bargain sale (part sale and part gift) of interests in property through a conservation easement and get the same kind of tax treatment as if you had made a bargain sale of the entire fee.

The Internal Revenue Code allows a charitable contribution deduction for the appraised value of rights donated for "conservation purposes" to public agencies or qualified charitable organizations. The tax code, at section 170(f)(3)(C) defines "conservation purposes" as:

(i) the preservation of land areas for public outdoor recreation or education or scenic enjoyment;
(ii) the preservation of historically important land areas or structures; or
(iii) the protection of natural environmental systems.

Landowners can receive a charitable deduction for the gift or bargain sale of an easement to a nonprofit organization only if the organization meets standards imposed by the Internal Revenue Service and described at section 501(c)(3) of the tax code. Basically, the IRS insists that both the donor and the receiving organization have conservation in mind. Thus, a gift of a conservation easement to The Nature Conservancy would probably be deductible, but a gift to a church probably would not.

At the time of its formation each charitable organization must have its tax status and eligibility to accept deductible gifts approved by the IRS. To be deductible, gifts of easements must be perpetual, binding forever anyone who owns the land. The recipient organization must be able to enforce the restrictions agreed upon and must agree never to sell, give away, or trade the rights received through the easement except to another conservation entity, which would agree to protect those rights in the same manner.

Going back to Harmony, Transylvania, for a moment, let's take a look at what happened regarding taxes to Betty Good's sister Jane when she decided to donate a conservation easement of her 10-acre share of Harmony Woods to the city.[8]

Tax Results from
Gift of Conservation Easement

Jane is 65 years old and was divorced some years ago. Like her sister Betty, she has a personal income of $37,000 a year and current itemized deductions of $4,000.

Jane's ten acres are not actually part of Harmony Woods, but the land borders the park and if developed, would degrade the park. Jane wants to keep the property as long as she lives, then give it to her daughter. However, she does not wish to see the land developed, and she fears that strong development pressure or increased property or estate taxes will force her to sell to a developer someday.

One day Mayor Doright asked Jane if she would donate a conservation easement over the land to the city. He explained that by doing so Jane could keep the land but would give up her rights to develop it. She could freeze the property's tax classification, reduce the taxable value of her gross estate for estate tax purposes, and be entitled to a present reduction of taxable income equal to the fair market value of the easement. Mayor Doright had an appraisal done, which showed the easement to be worth $7,000.

Results in terms of the year's spendable income may be illustrated in Table 3.

Easements, Assessors, and Property Tax Reductions

It might seem logical that a landowner who surrenders development rights for a public purpose should not pay taxes on the full earning potential of his property, usually cited as its "highest and best use." The assertion of this logic at county courthouses around the nation has received mixed reviews.

The personal attitudes of local officials and assessors are crucial in the decision as to whether property tax relief will be granted to someone whose property has been restricted through an easement. Some frankly don't believe that conservation is a public purpose. Others oppose any arrangement that reduces the local tax base. Still others wish to tax the holder of the easement because they claim the easement has "extinguished" development rights. According to this view, development rights frozen by an easement at a given property should force the holder of those rights to pay for the lost revenue.

The fundamental problem is less lofty. Assessors, who are paid to make assessments which will generate enough revenue to meet budgeted quotas, are apt to be skeptical of schemes that frustrate their purposes and are complicated to implement. Accordingly, a Wisconsin observer wrote in 1974, 13 years after Governor Nelson's easement program was launched, "There is no evidence that any Wisconsin assessor has recomputed a tax assessment on the basis of a newly sold conservation easement."[9]

The experience of one Maine landowner is common:

Peterson applied to have 100 acres of mixed wood classified as "forest land" for tax purposes (under the Maine Tree Growth Tax Law), to reduce his taxes on that parcel. Because the town was assessing at 100 percent, $24.40 (the state assessor's 100 percent per-acre valua-

125

Table 3—Tax Results from Gift of Conservation Easement

	INCOME WITHOUT DONATION	INCOME WITH DONATION
INCOME		
Adjusted gross income	$37,000	$37,000
Less: Excess itemized deductions and exemptions	(3,700)	(10,700)
Taxable income	$33,300	$26,300
TAXES		
Federal income tax (per tables)	$ 9,414	$ 6,459
State income tax (taxable income minus federal tax times 5 percent)	1,194	992
Total taxes	$10,608	$ 7,451
CASH RETURN		
Gross income	$37,000	$37,000
Less: Taxes	(10,608)	(7,451)
Net cash return after taxes	$26,392	$29,549
Value of gift to Jane		$ 3,157

tion for mixed wood in that county) would have become the new per-acre assessment for Peterson's forest land.

The assessor of Seaside, however, apparently viewed the Tree Growth Tax Law as an unwanted interference by the state in local affairs. He also apparently feared that the law would result in a substantial loss of revenue to the town. Peterson's application for forest land classification was denied, even though Peterson had complied with every requirement and the 100 acres met the definition of forest land. The assessor continued to tax the land at its fair market value.

Following receipt of the assessor's decision, Peterson appealed to the assessor as required by the law, and being unsuccessful, he then initiated a petition for reconsideration with the State Forestry Appeals Board. On appeal, the board ruled in Peterson's favor; the assessor had no valid grounds for denying classification of the parcel as timberland.[10]

Studies conducted in southern Illinois in the late sixties showed that assessors required by state law and Department of Revenue policy to assess rural properties according to the crop and timber productivity of each individual parcel, instead frequently did the simplest thing possible. They

126

either set an arbitrary "flat" rate on all unimproved land in their district, or—as 34 percent did—copied the figures from the preceding assessment period.[11]

All this is not meant to discourage grantors of easements from applying for reduced assessments or to impugn assessors, who, like appraisers, have understandable trouble evaluating abstractions such as the value of standing timber measured by the annual growth of trees. Plenty of reductions have been granted, and the situation should improve with experience. The following tips should help those who are applying for reduced assessments.

1. Don't assume that the assessment will be reduced automatically. You'll have to apply, probably in person.
2. It helps greatly if the assessor's obligation to consider the value of rights surrendered is clearly a matter of law. Take a copy of the statute with you. Some state easement statutes are very clear in this matter, such as the Colorado law cited below:

> Real property subject to one or more conservation easements in gross shall be assessed, however, with due regard to the restricted uses to which the property may be devoted. The valuation for assessment of a conservation easement which is subject to assessment and taxation, plus the valuation for assessment of lands subject to such easement, shall equal the valuation for assessment which would have been determined as to such lands if there were no conservation easement.[12]

(If the law is vague on the matter, ask your attorney to search for court cases which define the assessor's obligation.)

3. Also take a copy of the appraisal of the easement with you. Make sure the appraisal clearly states the value of each right surrendered.
4. Be prepared to appeal.

Enforcing the Terms of Easements

In perpetuity is a long time. Many treaties that were to endure "as long as the winds shall blow and as long as the grass shall grow" were not in force a century after they were signed. One must assume that over time the original force that inspired a landowner to restrict his property will dissipate, and that among all the individuals, groups, companies, and agencies that will ever own a piece of land, someone will challenge the terms of the easement. Any party serious about forever protecting ele-

127

ments of ecological diversity must be prepared for the challenge.

But what can one do? The problem is complex—part legal, part biological, and part social. Not only will owners change, but the biological material itself will change, according to genetic and ecological laws. A field now could become a forest in 50 years.

The best you can do is to make it as easy as possible for those who will monitor the easement over time to measure the extent of compliance. A preserve should be well designed *before* landowners are contacted. By the time you are ready to negotiate the specific terms and restrictions of an easement you should know at least:

1. Exactly what elements you wish to protect through the easement.
2. What they require to live at the site, both as species (if the elements are species) and in dynamic association with other living things.
3. What actions the owner might take that could jeopardize the vitality of these elements.
4. How you could devise a document that would establish your right to the elements and deny his ability to jeopardize them.

To know these things, you should obtain an aerial photograph of the general area you wish to protect. The photo can be used as a base map, against which you can outline, ideally through a series of transparent overlays, the boundaries of the species populations, vegetational communities and/or aquatic systems of greatest significance, property lines, existing structures, and the places where prior human disturbance is evident. This map should become part of the recorded easement document. Both parties should attest that the document describes fairly the condition of the land at the time the easement was created.

The original aerial photograph and subsequent photographs can be used to monitor changes on the land. In some states the entire landscape has been photographed from a plane at regular intervals. By consulting a complete photographic history, one can document changes humanly induced and perceive biological trends at the site.

It is important to monitor precisely the terms of the easement. In so doing, you should establish standard photographic monitoring and vegetation sampling points. Document the condition of the land at the time the easement is established and inspect the property at least annually, using the photos and sampling points to measure changes, induced either through natural processes or human intervention.

128

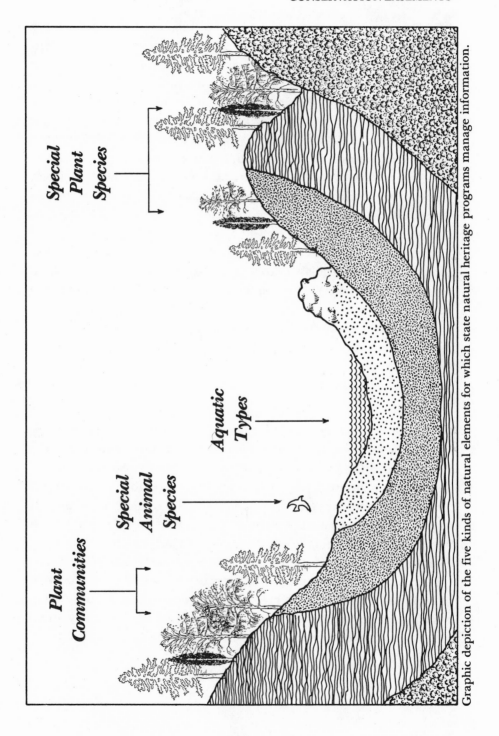

Special Plant Species

Aquatic Types

Special Animal Species

Plant Communities

Graphic depiction of the five kinds of natural elements for which state natural heritage programs manage information.

Document and monitor with greatest precision the extent and vitality of the natural elements you are trying to protect. Be sure you are able to know whether populations are declining or once-stable communities are transforming into something different. If you have to make changes in biological conditions at the site—say, to burn a prairie—be certain that the terms of the easement provide explicit permission to do so. There is a good body of case law upholding the rights of organizations and agencies to enforce the terms of easements held, but easement holders succeed only to the extent they can show the court the terms that are being violated.

The Nature Conservancy would prefer to stay out of court in managing its national preserve system and has endeavored to establish clear easement monitoring procedures. An excellent report of these procedures, entitled "Conservation Easement Resource Evaluation Procedures for The Nature Conservancy,"[13] is available from The Nature Conservancy, Eastern Regional Office, 294 Washington Street, Room 841, Boston, Massachusetts 02108.

The Conservancy insists, occasionally to the mild disgruntlement of its field staff, that each easement project must be documented in detail and approved by a flinty-eyed legal staff before a deed can be signed. So far, the group has not been challenged on any of its easements.

Summary

Conservation easements are restrictions that owners place on property. Agencies or private organizations, by holding easements, can control the owner's ability to destroy or degrade occurrences of natural elements. Easements can be either positive (allowing the holder to do something on the property), negative (restricting the owner from doing something on his property), appurtenant (benefiting a contiguous property), or in gross (benefiting the holder of the easement rather than a particular property). Easements can be in effect for a specific term or indefinitely.

Many states have recently passed progressive easement laws, allowing conservation organizations to hold perpetually easements in gross. Agencies and organizations could maximize the potential conceptually inherent in easements by applying them selectively to specific properties.

APPENDIX A

Sample Conservation Easement

THIS INDENTURE, made this _____ day of _____, 198____
WITNESSETH:

WHEREAS, _____ of _____, hereinafter called the Grantor, is the owner in fee simple of certain real property, hereinafter called the "Protected Property," which has aesthetic, scientific, educational and ecological value in its present state as a natural area which has not been subject to development or exploitation, which property is described as follows:
[Legal description of the land]

WHEREAS, [insert name of conservation organization or public body], hereinafter called the Grantee, is a [non-profit corporation incorporated under the laws of _____] or [public body] whose purpose is to [preserve and conserve natural areas for aesthetic, scientific, charitable and educational purposes]; and

WHEREAS, the Grantor and Grantee recognize the natural scenic, aesthetic and special character of the region in which the Protected Property is located, and have the common purpose of conserving the natural values of the Protected Property by the conveyance to the Grantee of a Conservation Easement on, over and across the Protected Property, which shall conserve the natural values of the Protected Property, conserve and protect the animal and plant populations, and prevent the use or development of that property for any purpose or in any manner which would conflict with the maintenance of the Protected Property in its natural, scenic and open condition for both this generation and future generations; and

WHEREAS, "aesthetic, scientific, educational and ecological value," "natural, scenic and open condition" and "natural values" as used herein shall, without limiting the generality of the terms, mean the condition of the Protected Property at the time of this grant, evidenced by reports, photographs, maps and scientific documentation possessed (at present or in the future) by the Grantee which the Grantee shall make available on any reasonable request to the Grantor, his heirs and assigns;

NOW THEREFORE, the Grantor, for and in consideration of the facts above recited and of the mutual convenants, terms, conditions and restrictions herein contained and as an absolute and unconditional gift does hereby give, grant, bargain, sell and convey unto the Grantee, its successors and assigns, forever a Conservation Easement in perpetuity over the Protected Property consisting of the following:

1. The right of view of the Protected Property in its natural, scenic, and open condition;
2. The right of the Grantee, in a reasonable manner and at reasonable times, to

enforce by proceedings at law or in equity the covenants hereinafter set forth, including but not limited to, the right to require the restoration of the Protected Property to the condition at the time of this grant. The Grantee, or its successors or assigns, does not waive or forfeit the right to take action as may be necessary to insure compliance with the covenants and purposes of this grant by any prior failure to act;

3. The right to enter the Protected Property at all reasonable times for the purpose of inspecting the Protected Property to determine if the Grantor, or his heirs or assigns, is complying with the covenants and purposes of this grant; and further to observe and study nature and to make scientific and educational observations and studies in such a manner as will not disturb the quiet enjoyment of the Protected Property by the Grantor, his heirs and assigns.

And in furtherance of the foregoing affirmative rights, the Grantor makes the following covenants, on behalf of himself, his heirs and assigns, which covenants shall run with and bind the Protected Property in perpetuity:

Covenants:* Without prior express written consent from the Grantee, on the Protected Property:

1. There shall be no construction or placing of buildings, camping accommodations or mobile homes, fences, signs, billboards or other advertising material, or other structures;

2. There shall be no filling, excavating, dredging, mining or drilling, removal of topsoil, sand, gravel, rock, minerals or other materials nor any building of roads or change in the topography of the land in any manner excepting the maintenance of foot trails;

3. There shall be no removal, destruction or cutting of trees or plants (except as is necessary to construct and maintain foot trails), planting of trees or plants, spraying with biocides, grazing of domestic animals or disturbance or change in the natural habitat in any manner;

4. There shall be no dumping of ashes, trash, garbage, or other unsightly or offensive material, and no changing of the topography through the placing of soil or other substance or material such as land fill or dredging spoils;

5. There shall be no manipulation or alteration of natural water courses, lake shores, marshes or other water bodies or activities or uses detrimental to water purity;

6. There shall be no operation of snowmobiles, dune-buggies, motorcycles, all-terrain vehicles or any other types of motorized vehicles;

7. There shall be no hunting or trapping except to the extent specifically approved by the Grantee as necessary to keep the animal population within the numbers consistent with the ecological balance of the area.

The Grantor, his heirs and assigns, agree to pay any real estate taxes or assessments levied by competent authorities on the Protected Property and to relieve the Grantee from responsibility for maintaining the Protected Property.

The Grantor agrees that the terms, conditions, restrictions, and purposes of this grant will be inserted by him in any subsequent deed, or other legal instrument, by which the Grantor divests himself of either the fee simple title to or his possessory interest in the Protected Property.

TO HAVE AND TO HOLD the said Conservation Easement unto the said Grantee, its successors and assigns forever.

Except as expressly limited herein, the Grantor reserves for himself, his heirs and assigns, all rights as owner of the Protected Property, including the right to use the property for all purposes not inconsistent with this grant.

The covenants agreed to and the terms, conditions, restrictions, and purposes imposed with this grant shall not only be binding upon the Grantor but also his agents, personal representatives, heirs and assigns, and all other successors to him in interest and shall continue as a servitude running in perpetuity with the Protected Property.

IN WITNESS WHEREOF the Grantor has set his hand the day and year first above written.

(Add acknowledgment form used in the State where the land is located.)

*Note: These clauses may be changed to meet specific variations and situations such as easements over farm lands where continued agricultural use or grazing is permitted; provision may also be made as appropriate for replacing existing buildings, maintaining access, or limited hunting. This sample is of a "Forever Wild" conservation easement.

APPENDIX B

A Good Easement Law

There is no ideal easement law on the books of any state at present. However, the following statute from Connecticut is an example of a clear and concise easement law. It provides that governmental agencies and conservation organizations alike can hold easements in gross and does not limit the duration of an easement to a specific term of years. The statute would be more useful to the grantor of an easement if it mandated that officials consider the value of easements when as-sessing property taxes.

DEEDS AND CONVEYANCES—CONSERVATION AND PRESERVATION RESTRICTIONS

SENATE BILL NO. 1647

PUBLIC ACT NO. 173

An Act concerning conservation and preservation restrictions.
Be it enacted by the Senate and House of Representatives in General Assembly convened:
Section 1.

For the purpose of this act, the following definitions shall apply: (a) "Conservation restriction" means a limitation, whether or not stated in the form of a restriction, easement, convenant or condition, in any deed, will or other instrument executed by or on behalf of the owner of the land described therein or in any order of taking such land whose purpose is to retain land or water areas predominantly in their natural, scenic or open condition or in agricultural, farming, forest or open space use. (b) "Preservation restriction" means a limitation, whether or not stated in the form of a restriction, easement, covenant or condition, in any deed, will or other instrument executed by or on behalf of the owner of land or in any order of taking of such land whose purpose is to preserve historically significant structures or sites.

Section 2.

No conservation restriction held by any governmental body or by a charitable corporation or trust whose purposes include conservation of land or water areas and no preservation restriction held by any governmental body or by a charitable corporation or trust whose purposes include preservation of buildings or sites of historical significance shall be unenforceable on account of lack of privity of estate or contract or lack of benefit to particular land or on account of the benefit being assignable or being assigned to any other governmental body or to any charitable corporation or trust with like purposes.

Section 3.

Such conservation and preservation restrictions are interests in land and may be acquired by any governmental body or any charitable corporation or trust which has the power to acquire interests in land in the same manner as it may acquire other interests in land. Such restrictions may be enforced by injunction or proceedings in equity.

Approved May 16, 1971.

CHAPTER ELEVEN

DEDICATION

Dedication as discussed here means the placement of a natural area into a legally established statewide system of nature preserves, whose member properties are protected by strong statutory language against condemnation or conversion to a different use. The preserve system is administered and usually managed by a state agency.

The agency can accept natural areas for dedication on behalf of the state through gift, transfers from another agency, or exchanges and can also purchase natural areas, within budgetary limits. Usually the only cost to the agency imposed by dedication is the expense of managing, posting, and sometimes fencing the preserves.

Landowners can dedicate specific interests in property as well as full fee title into a preserve system. For example, an owner could dedicate the rights to cut the trees in an old-growth stand while retaining the rights to live on or transfer his property. As with an easement, specific provisions of the arrangement can be tailored to suit individual circumstances. The terms of the arrangement are described in "articles of dedication" (see Appendix A), which are recorded with the clerk of the county in which the land is located.

The Strongest Tool

Dedication is the strongest protection tool discussed in this book, increasing protection offered even through fee acquisition in two ways. First, a county clerk cannot lawfully record articles of dedication unless they contain terms protecting the land against modification or encroachment. Secondly, all nature preserves acts contain clear language protecting dedicated properties against condemnation or conversion. The Ohio statute is typical in stating that:

> Dedicated areas shall not be taken for any other use except another public use after a finding by the Department of Natural Resources of the existence of an imperative and unavoidable public necessity for such other public use and with the approval of the governor. Except as may otherwise be provided in the articles of dedication, the department may grant, upon such terms and conditions as it may de-

137

termine, an estate, interest or right in, or dispose of, a nature preserve, but only after a finding by the department of the existence of
an imperative and unavoidable public necessity for such grant or dis-
position and with the approval of the Governor.[1]

There must be a public notice and opportunity for public hearing before the above findings can be made. South Carolina, Kentucky, Indiana,
Illinois, Iowa, North Dakota, Kansas, and Mississippi statutes also declare
that dedicated preserves are "at their highest and best use for public benefit." (The Mississippi Statute appears as Appendix A, Chapter Twelve.)

Suppose then that the Ohio State Department of Transportation
sought to run a new highway along a route that passed through an Ohio
Nature Preserve. The DOT could not carry out its plan unless the Department of Natural Resources, the agency which administers the nature preserves system, found that the siting of the highway through the preserve
was an "unavoidable and imperative public necessity," and the governor
agreed. Furthermore, the department would have to notify the general
public of the plan and provide an opportunity for a public hearing. From
a practical standpoint, if the governor and DNR (whose director is employed at the governor's pleasure) were disposed to sacrifice a preserve,
strong public opposition could be the deciding factor.

By contrast, the state would find it easier to condemn an area owned by
a conservation agency or organization and managed for natural values
but not dedicated legally as a nature preserve.

Should litigation be necessary to prevent the state from attempting to
convert a nature preserve to another public use, the chances are excellent
that citizens' groups could achieve legal standing as plaintiffs (since the
preserves are held in trust for public benefit), and given the clarity and
force of the enabling language, chances for success in the suit would be
good.

Using Dedication in a
State Natural Areas Program

In the early 1960s individuals in Illinois, aware that repeated clearing
of the forests and tillage of the prairies had all but destroyed the state's
ecological heritage, sought a strong means to protect what was left. They
came up with the idea of a system of nature preserves, carefully selected
and protected with all the strength the general assembly would allow.

Their ideas, expressed in the Illinois Nature Preserves Act of 1963, have since been imitated and modified in 11 other states (see Appendix B), including several other states in the Midwest, where there seems to be a regional awareness of the value of what has been lost and a special determination to protect the remainder.

In building preserves systems, state officials must choose carefully which areas are important enough to protect forever for the people of the state, to shelter from property taxes if privately owned, and to obligate their agencies to manage. Seven of the 12 states with dedication statutes use state natural heritage inventories to identify areas possessing the most significant natural values. Sound judgment rests upon the availability of comparative information, such as the relative rarity and degree of protection enjoyed by the plants, animals, natural communities, and ecosystems that occur in the state. Several state natural area programs have cited as an ultimate goal the representation of good examples of all elements of their state's natural diversity within a system of dedicated nature preserves.

Many areas have been dedicated in order to strengthen already existing protection. The states such as Illinois, Indiana, and Ohio, which have well-established preserve systems have dedicated many natural areas owned by state agencies, universities, and private organizations such as The Nature Conservancy. The Nature Conservancy has allowed many of its preserves to be dedicated in order to strengthen their protection through state law.

Apparently there has been only one serious challenge to a dedicated nature preserve. This occurred in Indiana, where a county government sought to take about 1/10 acre within a nature preserve for a bridge approach. This move was opposed by the private conservation organization that owned the property in fee but was supported by the Nature Preserves Commission and the governor, who were prepared to declare the bridge an imperative and unavoidable public necessity. When the case went to public hearing, the hearing officer directed the parties to seek an acceptable compromise. A way was finally found to build the bridge without disturbing the preserve.

Taxes and Dedication

Income Taxes. Many landowners have taken advantage of tax incentives described in chapter 170(F)(3)(b) of the Internal Revenue Code by donating development rights through conservation easements to charita-

139

ble organizations or public agencies, then writing off the taxable value of the development rights (see Chapter Ten).

It is not yet certain whether the IRS would construe rights conveyed through articles of dedication as similarly deductible. At this writing no individual who has dedicated either full fee title or rights to property has applied to the IRS for a deduction.

The ability of landowners to receive tax benefits for property dedicated would fill a special protection gap in states such as Kentucky or Mississippi, which do not have conservation easement statutes, but which have strong nature preserves acts. There, owners could donate specific property rights through articles of dedication but not through easements in gross.

The few tax attorneys who have considered the deductibility of articles of dedication seem to agree they would be treated by the IRS as conservation easements since they serve the same purpose as easements and, if anything, restrict property rights to an even greater degree than easements. To date, state officials have not encouraged private property owners to dedicate their land, regardless of how significant these properties might be. In fact, only a handful of the more than 200 areas that have been dedicated in the United States are owned privately by individuals, and none of the owners has applied for a charitable deduction.

Some state officials contend that people would sell or donate the property before they would dedicate it. They believe that no sane individual would want to possess a deed so severely and permanently restricted. Still, these restrictions offer certainty and stability to landowners who would prefer that their property remain as a natural area. Given the economic incentives to develop land, many areas are undisturbed only because such people have already made sacrifices.

Some officials feel that, like easements, restrictive terms contained in articles of dedication will be hard to enforce. Sons and daughters, it is argued, will be tempted to cut and sell the old trees that their parents loved. New owners, having no emotional attachment to the property, will sue the Nature Preserves Commission, challenge the statute, or, worse still, simply develop the property and force the state to take action.

However, all nature preserve statutes express forcefully the intent of the state to protect forever certain precious places. It would seem that articles of dedication clearly drafted, describing conditions on the land that are clearly documented, would be upheld if specific terms were violated.

Property Taxes. Most nature preserves acts provide for relief from property taxes equal to the assessed value of the right surrendered. In Ohio alone dedicated properties are completely exempted from property taxes. As discussed in the previous chapter, the attitudes of county assessors toward reduced assessment varies widely. In all cases it is up to the landowner to apply for the reduction. It helps if the statute clearly requires assessors to consider the differences between the value of the whole fee title and the rights surrendered through dedication, as is the case in Kentucky and Mississippi.

Trust Dedication. "Trust dedication" is used here to mean dedication as described above with one important difference. In this case a trust is created by law and administered by a designated agency. Natural areas are dedicated into the trust, rather than into a nature preserves system.

There is only one example in the United States, namely the South Carolina Heritage Trust, established by the South Carolina Heritage Trust Act of 1976.[2] The standard for permitting a change in the use of the property is the same as with other dedication statutes ("imperative and unavoidable public necessity"), but in South Carolina the decision as to whether the change would be allowed is made by a court of law rather than by an administrative agency. The agency and the governor still have to make their findings, and the public hearing still must take place, but a court makes the final decision.

The statute creates a broad but definite set of trust beneficiaries. To quote the language used in the South Carolina statute:

> The beneficiaries of this trust are and shall be the present and future generations of citizens of the state, more particularly those present and future citizens residing within a close proximity to any area or feature which itself, or an interest therein, becomes, constitutes, or comprises a part of the corpus of such trust and who actually enjoy use of such area or feature; and further and more particularly, those present and future students, teachers, and persons residing in the state who are concerned with conservation or with research in any facet of ecology, history, or archaeology and who actually utilize any such area or feature for the promotion of such interest, (Section 9).

The assumption here is that these neighbors, students, teachers, and concerned citizens would be the parties-plaintiff before the court in a case where the court must decide whether or not the property is to be preserved.

141

As of this writing only two areas have been dedicated into the South Carolina Heritage Trust, and neither has been challenged.

Further Implications of Dedication as a Concept

The potential of dedication as a protection tool is enormous. For instance, a group of private citizens and public officials are striving to create a "water preserve system" in Colorado, where first claim to the use of water in a stream is nearly as important as outright fee ownership of property. Under this arrangement senior water rights could be dedicated into a preserve system in order to leave water in streams, especially during the dry periods when the cumulative legal claims can draw a stream bed dry.

The idea has been slow in implementation, mainly because Colorado courts have yet to decide definitely whether anyone can exercise a water right in order to leave water in a stream (according to Colorado water rights law, it must be applied to a "beneficial" use, which has meant traditionally an economic use such as irrigation). Until a legal preserve system can be established, the Colorado chapter of The Nature Conservancy is purchasing senior water rights to streams supporting significant vegetation or fauna, and reselling them to the Colorado Water Conservation Board for management.[3]

Summary

The dedication of significant areas into a legal system of nature preserves protects elements of natural diversity against all private and most public development initiatives. The concept is especially well established in the Midwest, where there are several well-developed nature preserves systems.

In most enabling statutes, owners of properties dedicated are awarded some degree of relief from property taxation, but the federal income tax consequences of dedication, though promising, are as yet untested. In South Carolina significant properties are dedicated into a legal trust, rather than an administrative system. Colorado citizens and officials are attempting to establish a preserves system into which water rights could be dedicated.

APPENDIX A
SAMPLE ARTICLES OF DEDICATION

Dedication of a Nature Preserve

Lake Defiance

KNOW ALL MEN BY THESE PRESENTS, that the *State of Illinois, Department of Conservation,* being the owner thereof does hereby dedicate the following described real property as a nature preserve:

Parcel 1: Part of the East Half of Section 1, Township 44 North, Range 8 East of the Third Principal Meridian, and part of the West Half of Section 6, Township 44 North, Range 9 East of the Third Principal Meridian, all described as follows: Beginning at the Southwest Corner of the Southeast Quarter of the Northeast Quarter of said Section 1, thence East 150 feet, thence North 960 feet to a point, thence East 130 feet to a point, thence North 200 feet to a point, thence North 65° East 720 feet to a point, thence East 1,000 feet to a point, thence North 45° East 400 feet to a point, thence East 380 feet to a point, thence South 30° West 480 feet to a point, thence South 55° East 300 feet to a point, thence South 1,180 feet to a point on the Center Line of said Section 6, thence Westerly 1,230 feet along said Center Line to a point, thence South 240 feet to a point, thence South 40° West 1,220 feet to a point, thence South 86° West 710 feet to a point, thence North 22° West 220 feet to a point, thence North 21° East 1,100 feet to a point on the Center Line of said Section 1, thence Westerly 200 feet along said Center Line to the Point of Beginning, in McHenry County, Illinois.

The property heretofore described is dedicated for the purposes, and shall be held, maintained, and used, as provided for Nature Preserves, in "An Act in relation to the acquisition, control, maintenance, improvement and protection of State parks and nature preserves," approved June 26, 1925, as heretofore amended and "An Act relating to the creation of the Illinois Nature Preserves Commission and defining its powers and duties," approved August 28, 1963, as heretofore amended. Said property is further dedicated for the purposes, and shall be held, maintained, and used, as provided for Nature Preserves in any amendment to said Acts enacted hereafter, but no such amendment shall alter the exclusive commitment of said land to the preservation of natural conditions for the purposes specified in said Acts as of the date of this dedication.

APPENDIX B

Dedication
A Look at the State Laws

	Date Established	Number of Preserves	Number of Acres	Property Tax Relief
Arkansas	1973	17	3,399	No reference in statute
Delaware	1978	0	0	No reference in statute
Illinois	1963	68	17,149.5	Illinois revenue law says articles easement for taxes
Indiana	1967	51	7,270	No reference in statute
Iowa	1965	54	3,500	None
Kansas	1974	0	0	No reference in statute
Kentucky	1976	4	1,305	The value of interests so dedicated shall be exempt from property
Mississippi	1978	2	362	Committee-owned lands exempt, privately-owned lands entitled to assessment based on reduced value
North Dakota	1975	2	210	No reference in statute
Ohio	1970	45	37	Complete exemption
Oregon	1979	2	about 900	Indirectly, through an open space assessment law
South Carolina	1976	3	22,400	No reference in statute

Key for Protection Against Condemnation or Conversion
1-Dedicated lands are declared by law to be at their highest and best use for public benefit
2-Standard against condemnation or conversion of "unavoidable and/or imperative public necessity," as found or approved by:

a) Administrative agency
b) Governor
c) Another body

d) An act of the legislature
e) The Department of Natural Resources

144

	Agency with Staff Function	Agency with Advisory Board	Protection Against Condemnation or Conversion
Arkansas	Arkansas Natural Heritage Commission staff	*Arkansas Natural Heritage Commission	2a, 3, 4
Delaware	DNR, Office of Heritage Programming & Research	*Delaware Natural Areas Advisory Council	2b, 2d, 2e, 3
Illinois	Illinois Nature Preserves Commission staff	*Illinois Nature Preserves Commission	1, 2a, 2b, 2e, 3
Indiana	DNR, Division of Nature Preserves	*Indiana Natural Resources Commission	1, 2a, 2b, 3
Iowa	State Preserves Advisory Board staff	*State Preserves Advisory Board	1, 2a, 2b, 2c, 3
Kansas	Kansas State Park & Resources Authority	Kansas Scientific & Natural Areas Advisory Board	1, 2d, 3
Kentucky	Kentucky Heritage Program	*Kentucky Nature Preserves Commission	1, 2a 3 (notice only)
Mississippi	Mississippi Natural Heritage Program	*Mississippi Wildlife Heritage Committee	1, 2a, 2
North Dakota	North Dakota Department of Parks & Recreation	A body consisting of directors of various state agencies	1, 2a&b, 3
Ohio	Ohio DNR, Division of Natural Area Preserves	Ohio Natural Areas Council	2b, 2e, 3
Oregon	Natural Heritage Advisory Council	State Land Board	1, 2a, 3
South Carolina	South Carolina Heritage Trust Program	*Heritage Trust Advisory Board	1, 5

3-Public notice and opportunity for hearing required by law, before such findings can be made
4-Dedicated natural areas declared to be areas of local significance under 4 (f) of the Dept. of Transportation Act of 1966
5-Dedicated areas are held in public trust, removable only by judicial proceeding

*Body with primary authority to approve dedication of nature preserves

CHAPTER TWELVE

LOBBYING

The ability to lobby persuasively is a very important factor in a state's attempt to preserve its ecological heritage. Several of the tools discussed so far—most notably dedication and conservation easements—are created through state law, and appropriations for land acquisition funds are granted by the legislature. In some states even heritage programs have been created through an act of state law. Thus it is no surprise that conservation leaders—people with professional backgrounds in wildlife management, botany, or business administration—find themselves spending more and more time at statehouses these days, struggling to pass protection laws and secure budget appropriations.

They find that lobbying is hard work. Money, authority, and manpower are popular prizes not easily won. In a tight budget your gain is someone else's loss, and your simple idea—a nature preserves act or a cigarette tax to finance land acquisition—is apt to be opposed by factions whose members don't even take the trouble to understand it.

Furthermore, each legislator confronts thousands of bills each session, each of which is desperately important to someone who will compete with you for the collective ear of the state general assembly.

This chapter will present a basic crash course for nonprofessional lobbyists, something helpful to read on the way to the statehouse. The discussion will begin by considering how to prepare a good lobbying effort, will pass through the basic steps in the legislative process, and conclude with a detailed chronological account of a successful attempt to pass a fine natural areas protection act in Mississippi.[1]

One note of caution: The Internal Revenue Service regulates the extent to which publicly supported, nonprofit charities can engage in lobbying, mainly by setting limits on the percentage of their operating budgets such groups can devote to lobbying without risking their tax exempt status. The precise percentage formula appears in the Internal Revenue Code at section 501(H).

Preparing an Effort

Starting Early. Time is of the essence in lobbying. The longer you wait, the more problems you create for yourself. A legislative session is like a desert flower after a rainstorm, blossoming brilliantly for a moment—usually 30 or 60 work days*—then withering at once. You should be prepared when the session opens.

A good rule of thumb is to start organizing at least three months before the legislative session opens. There are many practical reasons for starting so early, both in terms of the legislative schedule and your ability to organize support. Most states now provide for interim committee meetings (between sessions) and prefiling of bills. (You can drop a bill in the hopper in July for January consideration.) As a result, the legislative calendar may already be crowded with bills that have been studied, testified on, and reported out of committee by the second day of the new session. If you start to organize when the session opens, you'll find that the drafting office is busy, that committees are already meeting, and that lawmakers are occupied. Give yourself some breathing room. A legislator who could have spent a leisurely hour or two reading over your bill and asking questions during the first month of the session will be entirely unapproachable as the session draws to a close. A legislator who does not fully understand a bill and who does not have the time to research his questions (as is usually the case toward the end of the session) is almost instinctively inclined to cover himself by voting against it.

It takes time to organize support, which should be as broad as possible, ideally drawing together business interests and conservationists. You might need a month just to meet your key legislative supporters and get them together with citizen leaders and support groups.

Sometimes you can help yourself before the session opens by getting the purpose of your bill adopted as a plank in the platform of the dominant political party. Party leaders are most accessible and favors are most easily granted during preparation of the party platform, a document created merely to attract the support of a broad range of interests. It is sometimes easy to discuss your objective with members of the party platform committee, the group responsible for drafting the platform. Try to persuade

---

*Most state legislatures meet annually, but many stagger long and short sessions (frequently 60 and 30 days) every other year. These states concentrate on passing the budget in the long session and discuss supplements to the budget during the brief session. At this writing 13 state legislatures meet *only* every other year unless, in most instances, the governor calls a special session in the off-year. (See Appendix A for a state-by-state breakdown.)

them to endorse as a plank a statement of your bill's objectives, drafted as closely as possible to the actual language of your bill. Don't hesitate to remind party members of your plank throughout the campaign.

Organizing support is mostly a matter of educating people. The legislator to whom you are introducing yourself has probably never heard of you, and he almost certainly doesn't know what you're talking about. You'll have to tell him how your bill will help him and his constituents. In fact, you'll have to remind him, perhaps repeatedly during your campaign, that many of your supporters *are* his constituents. Unless you command a great deal of influence, or have a lot of favors to collect, you'll probably need some indication of broad support, through memberships or user groups, to persuade some legislators.

If you're well versed before you go in to meet him, you'll probably make a good impression. If he appears receptive, ask his advice on strategic matters. Don't be shy. You or some other member of your group will have to be directly responsible for the effort to pass your bill. Someone will have to shepherd the bill through the entire process described below and must be available to provide expert advice and general leadership at a moment's notice. Murphy's Law applies with a vengeance to lobbying. Because the process of passing a bill is long and requires the constant cooperation of disparate groups of people, many things can go wrong. Assume they will and be prepared.

Sources of Information on the Legislative Process in Your State. To lobby well, you must understand the legislative process in your state. The *state constitution, state statutes, state regulations,* and the *legislative rules* (rules of each separate house and joint rules, which govern procedural aspects of both houses) are the fundamental documents that describe the organization and basic duties of legislatures. They grant legislative power and describe the limits of legislative authority. The constitution, state statutes, and state regulations should each have a section devoted to the legislature, where you can find the duties of the presiding officer, the time and days for meeting, and often a description of the committee structure.

The legislative rules present the specific guidelines by which legislatures function daily. The rules provide for a specific organizational structure and govern parliamentary procedure, committee structure, and the duties of committees and chairmen. For example, many states have adopted a system of deadlines by which time a bill must be introduced, or reported from committee action, or have received floor action. If a bill misses one of these it is no longer eligible for consideration. Obviously, you have to know these deadlines, and you can find them in the legislative rules. In many states the League of Women Voters publishes a manual about the state legislature, designed to identify the members and clarify procedures for those who will be working with legislators.

What You Should Know Before You Begin. First you have to know the cast of characters, especially (1) potential supporters, (2) committee chairmen, (3) legislative leaders, (4) the key people in the executive branch of government, and (5) beyond the group with whom you will work actively, your potential friends and adversaries and the lobbyists who represent them, if they are organized as a group. Ours may be a government of laws, but people make, enforce, and interpret the laws.

Learn to recognize the strengths and weaknesses of all these people. Find out what they think of you and your bill, if anything. If your supporters have managed to alienate or remain unknown to an influential faction in either house, plan to cultivate the support of its leaders.

It is sometimes a good idea to obtain the sponsorship or cosponsorship of someone who generally opposes the kind of proposal that you're making. If, for example, you are trying to obtain money for a land acquisition program, it may be wise to seek the support of someone who typically opposes virtually all new spending and frequently opposes environmental legislation. The sponsorship of such a person provides a signal to his traditional allies that your bill is somehow exceptional and it is all right to vote for it. Legislators frequently look to certain colleagues for leadership, especially when they have not had time to properly research or evaluate the bill on its merits.

Get to know the presiding officer in each house and discover their positions on your bill at the earliest possible moment. (Caution: A "position" —how a legislator votes—may differ from the way he feels personally about an issue. The "position" is the important part.) If the presiding officer opposes your bill, or has not yet formed an opinion, canvass your allies to find people who know him. Ask them to explain the bill and request a favorable committee referral.

Learn to recognize true leadership. Some members, such as weak committee chairmen, possess nominal rather than real power. Political leaders are frequently the most powerful members, regardless of their office.

Also, each legislature contains members whose judgment and integrity command respect even though they wield relatively little political or official power. Especially in moments of uncertainty, legislators turn to colleagues possessing personal qualities of leadership.

Recognize the interest groups within the legislature. If an influential legislator is mesmerized by a group opposed to your bill, try to find some way to break the spell. Learn which legislators are beholden to which interest groups and where each key interest group is apt to stand on your bill.

Know those legislators who oppose your bill, and, more important, why they oppose it. A legislator may have close ties to an opponent or he may oppose your basic objective or he may perceive something distasteful about the way your bill is phrased. The first problem can be neutralized, but you should probably forget about the second unless you have plenty of time. The third probably can be overcome with a simple language amendment.

Compromise. Compromise, like it or not, defines the legislative process. A legislature exists to transform many vectors of public opinion into a rough consensus.

In negotiating, you must know what is essential to you and what is not. Never compromise your basic objective, but if you have to, it pays to consider reasonable, constructive compromise on nonessential points. Your willingness to bend when you can may establish your credibility with legislators. Legislators are likely to appreciate your willingness to make life easier for them, particularly during the frenzied moments of a session. Once established, your foundation of credibility will support you year after year.

Patience is an invaluable asset. Often it takes several years to pass a bill. If things are not going well for your bill this session and your bill is transforming before your eyes into something alien to you, you might be wise to withdraw it while you can. Work this year to build support and educate legislators and reintroduce it next year.

Working with Legislators. Lawmakers are quite human, but in the press of business many seem to have adapted a special set of antennae that allows them to sense quickly what you want and have to offer. Be honest with them, even if you have to risk losing ground when answering a pointed question. You can earn a lifelong enemy by providing incorrect or unreliable information, particularly if the misinformation results in a leg-

151

islator's embarrassment. If you provide information and later find out it is incorrect, quickly inform the legislator of your mistake. Ideally, you should be esteemed as a reliable source and consulted frequently for an opinion about your field of expertise.

Learn to keep a secret. Never repeat a confidential statement of one legislator to another legislator, a lobbyist, a friend, or to the press. Still, find out all you can. Legislators have inside information, especially about their colleagues. They know who knows whom and who is affiliated with whom and what certain of their cohorts are apt to think of your bill. When you are conducting strategy sessions with your colleagues, caution them to keep the proceedings in confidence. Also, if the press contacts you for a statement on your bill, restrict your statement to your position or that of your group. Don't mention a legislator or his position unless he has authorized you to do so. Even with that permission, find out first exactly what you can say, so that you can defend any statement you make.

Be willing to do legwork for those legislators who support you. Despite what you may have heard, state legislators are overworked and under-staffed. Be willing to save them time by writing summaries of your bill, re-searching relevant matters (such as the fiscal impact of your bill), inform-ing a committee or being available for consultation during floor debate. Offer to prepare letters or memos for them. Letters written on a legisla-tor's stationery are usually your best bet for credibility. (Of course, the legislator should always approve their distribution.)

Count upon the lawmakers supporting your bill to help you with their colleagues. Credit their successes but don't damn their failures. And when success arrives, make sure their constituents know about it. Always make a copy for the legislator whenever you send out a relevant letter, memo, or article. This lets him know you appreciate his help, that you are thinking of him, that he's invaluable. These copies will give him points back home. These items should be basically matters of common sense.

Stages in the Legislative Process
The basic stages of the legislative process are: Content preparation, drafting, introduction, referral, committee action, floor action, confer-ence action, and executive action.

Preparing the Content of a Bill. As you prepare the content of your bill, work with as many groups and individuals as possible, but make sure your supporters agree about what is desired before you ask a legislator to introduce your bill. The ideas and procedures involved should be clearly defined and commonly understood. The group must present a united front to the legislature, regardless of differences that may have occurred during preparation. A legislator looking for a reason to vote against the bill can point to divisions within your ranks.

Those preparing the content should anticipate arguments and gather evidence to counteract the opponents. Ideally, the sponsoring legislators should be involved at this point to predict how their colleagues will react to potentially controversial aspects of the bill. If you can't get the sponsors, invite an insider to meet with the preparing group.

Know exactly how influential state resource agencies are with the governor. There is usually an individual on the governor's personal staff assigned as a liaison to the natural resource agencies, responsible for monitoring their activities. That person will be aware of every bill proposed that could affect natural resource policy and will probably recommend at some point that the governor either support or oppose your bill. It is essential to meet this person at a very early date, to discuss your bill informally, and to receive some sense of the governor's potential reaction.

Sponsorship and Drafting of the Language. The ideal sponsor of your bill is usually the chairman of the committee to which the bill will be referred. Whoever it is, the sponsor must be trusted and respected by his peers. He must understand the legislative process and must be genuinely interested in the bill.

Commitment is the key. If you have to choose, it is usually better to have your bill sponsored by an able but not particularly powerful member who cares personally about the bill and will devote primary attention to it than to attract the casual and lethargic sponsorship of a powerful member. Try to get as many sponsors as possible because sponsorship indicates support. You're probably in trouble if you have but one green sponsor's name on the bill. In such a case you might withdraw your bill for now.

Some legislatures have joint committees composed of members of both houses. In such states it may be dangerous to enlist for the same bill sponsors from different houses because the sponsors may fight over which house ultimately gets credit for passage of the bill. If there is a joint committee system, assess the situation carefully before you choose a sponsor. Sometimes it is wise to choose a sponsor from whichever house is apt to give you the most trouble, since a senator may well be swayed by the sponsorship of another senator. Other times you'll choose someone from the more promising chamber since passage in one house creates a momentum for the second house.

Your bill must be well drafted. An ambiguous sentence, a word incorrectly used, or a paragraph that contradicts a provision of the state constitution can spell defeat, and every amendment offered on the floor is a potential crisis. Each legislature has a fulltime drafting staff, consisting of attorneys and other professionals who work for one house, both houses, or a committee of a house. In some states major political parties have drafters as well.

Because the drafting staff usually can draft bills only at the request of a legislator, you have to ask the sponsor to arrange an appointment for you with a member of the drafting staff. When you meet, first explain the intent and purposes of the bill, then discuss specific wording. If possible, have your group's attorney provide, informally, a first draft of the bill that you want drafted. It is also a good idea to explain each part of the bill in the margins of the first draft and provide this to both the sponsor and the drafting office.

Arrange with the legislator to have the staff drafter send you a copy of his work so that you can review it and suggest final changes. Good drafting helps you avoid a lot of problems. Many people overlook this very critical part of the process.

Introduction. After the bill is drafted, it is introduced. Only a legislator can introduce a bill.

Referral to Committee. In most states the lieutenant governor refers bills to senate committees and the speaker of the house refers bills to committees of the house of representatives. In some states the president *pro tempore* of the senate refers senate bills. Favorable referral is very important. A presiding officer who opposes your bill and does not mind being arbitrary can refer the bill to a committee from which he knows it will never emerge favorably reported.

It helps to make an appointment with the presiding officer, if possible through the primary sponsor, to meet for a few minutes and explain the nature, content, and purpose of the bill. The sponsor may be able to take care of this without a meeting.

Committee Action. Committee action is the heart of the legislative process. Most decisions affecting the content of a bill are made in committee. A bill is rarely considered on the floor without a favorable committee report (although some legislative rules allow for what is called "a discharge petition and consideration on a minority report").

The ultimate glory is to have an unchanged bill favorably reported from committee. Depending upon the nature and complexity of the bill, this is quite possible.

After your bill has been referred to a committee but before the committee members consider it officially, there is usually a public hearing on the bill. Now is the time to rally your troops. Have as many supporters as possible express themselves, and be sure to orchestrate their remarks. Your leaders should spend a few minutes with each committee member to explain the bill. Ask the chairman when he plans to call the bill up before the committee and plan to be present. If you are permitted, try to attend any caucuses or committee markup sessions to assist the sponsor. This is especially important should any questions arise during the markup that the sponsor cannot answer immediately, as frequently happens when committee members first begin to look at the actual language of the bill. Someone must be there who knows the bill and who can respond with authority.

Ask if you may make a brief presentation to the committee as a group —and keep it brief. If objections to the bill arise either in the individual meetings or in the committee, be willing to work out a compromise amendment that does not sacrifice your basic objective.

It is far better to amend a bill in committee than on the floor, where there are more members and consequently more opinions. Legislators are apt to follow the committee's recommendation on a fairly noncontroversial bill. If you have to amend a bill, offer to work with the legislators requesting the amendment and with the drafting staff in drawing up the amendment.

Sometimes when the amendment is presented, someone will voice another objection, and you'll have to go through the whole thing again. This may happen two or three times, so be patient—normally it will happen only once because most objections are voiced in one session and can be resolved in a second session.

Should you encounter a committee chairman who states that he does not plan to call your bill up for the committee's attention, you have a real problem. Some legislatures allow only the chairman to call up a bill.

Others permit the vice-chairman to do so; others a majority of the committee members (again, consult your legislative rules). In this situation talk to the principal sponsor before you decide what to do. You may elect to have the bill reported from committee in the other house rather than buck the chairman. That way the bill can come back to a different committee with a more tolerant chairman after it passes the other house.

Generally, resolve all possible problems in committee. When a committee chairman declares to the full house that his committee has "perfected" your bill, the members can revel in the knowledge that a thoroughbred rather than a nag has come before them. On the other hand, you've got trouble when dissident committee members attack the bill on the floor and begin to recite the points of controversy before the full house. Be ready to fight.

Floor Action. Floor action follows committee action. If you worked hard when the bill was in committee, floor action should be easy, provided the bill is not too complex or controversial.

After committee action, assess your chances. If necessary, talk to as many members of the house as possible, one at a time. At this point supportive legislators can help immensely because you won't have enough time to talk to all the legislators. Supporters can contact their colleagues, explain the bill, obtain assurances of support, swap votes if necessary, and generally relieve your burden. However, if your well-placed allies report that you have no problems, go to a movie or an unpopular bar. There is no need to risk raising issues in conversation that have not bothered legislators so far. "If it ain't broke, don't fix it."

Should trouble develop on the floor, have a prearranged plan for the chairman or person handling the bill to lay it on the table "subject to call" until you can talk to the opponents and resolve the problem. In many states a motion merely to "lay on the table" kills the bill because the rules state that a bill cannot be removed from the table. Your colleagues might be upset to find that their bill has become affixed to the table for the rest of the session. Thus "lay on the table *subject to call*." Again, know the rules in your state.

In both floor action and committee action, keep a headcount of yeas and nays to gauge your bill's chances of passage and to monitor support and opposition. If the bill fails once, you will know whom you have to woo and whose support could waver in the next session. Always be present in the chamber whenever the bill could conceivably come up for debate. Questions may arise that the chairman or the person handling the bill cannot answer and you may be asked for information. A nod of your head or a thumb across the nose from the gallery could indicate whether a proposed amendment is satisfactory or not. The legislator will depend on your expertise at this time.

After floor approval in one house, the bill is sent to the other house for consideration. The processes can be the same in both houses or they can be completely different.

In some states, for example, the smaller of the two houses votes on bills through majority party caucuses, and you must have an ally in that caucus. Learn the rules.

If the second house approves the bill exactly as it was approved by the first house, the bill proceeds to the governor for his signature. If the second house approves the bill in a different form, the bill is returned to the first house to see if the members agree with the changes. If they do, the bill proceeds to the governor. If they don't, the bill is sent to a joint conference committee of the two houses. The first two contingencies—approval of an identical bill and joint approval of an amended bill—present no problem. The third contingency imposes one more hurdle.

Conference. Conference committees usually consist of two to four members representing the majority view of their respective houses. They are asked to resolve the differences between the two houses. Normally, conference committees can discuss only disputed matters, but sometimes they are allowed to rewrite the entire bill—check the legislative rules. Conference committees are usually under pressure to produce a bill of some kind because it is often late in the session and because both houses have already approved some form of the bill. Compromise is the grist of conference committees. Once the committee agrees upon a bill, it goes to each house for a vote. The vote can normally be only to accept or reject the compromise.

Executive Action. After legislative approval, the bill is sent to the governor for executive action. Some few states, such as North Carolina, have no executive action. There, after approval by the second house, the bill becomes law. By the time your bill reaches this point, you should know what the governor will do since you long ago made it a point to determine the position of his natural resource advisors. You have already drafted or

amended the bill to eliminate their objections, if possible. Thus, a gubernatorial veto is unnecessary. The executive staffers should have been consulted and included throughout the entire process.

If the governor insists upon compromises that defeat your objectives,
get the bill passed, then generate public and legislative pressure to have
him sign it. Again, never compromise the heart of your bill.

Case Study:
How the Mississippi Natural Heritage Act of 1978 Became Law

Following is a chronological history of the passage of Senate Bill 2261,
Mississippi State Legislature, regular session of 1978. The legislation, entitled "The Mississippi Natural Heritage Act of 1978," establishes procedures for voluntary registration or dedication of significant natural areas
which have been identified by the Mississippi Natural Heritage Program.
Despite its importance, the act is not terribly complicated. Its simple form
facilitated its passage.

This chronology should provide insight into how a bill becomes law.
Passage of this heritage act was fairly typical. The bill was navigated
through several crises—including floor amendments, a subtle challenge
by the executive branch, and rereferrals between committees—before it
burst into the sunshine of the Mississippi code.

The "I" in this account is Rick Fortenberry, a Mississippi attorney
whose previous experience as the director of the Legislative Services Office
of the Mississippi State Legislature served him well at the helm. At the
time Mr. Fortenberry worked as the director of the Mississippi field office
of The Nature Conservancy.

October 1977. I received information from The Nature Conservancy's
national office about desired heritage legislation. Included was material
on registration, dedication, and other tools and copies of statutes from
other states. I reviewed this information and prepared my own draft to
use as a basis for forthcoming discussions in Arlington, Virginia.

November 16, 1977. I spent the afternoon with The Nature Conservancy staff members in Arlington, reviewing, amending, and arguing
over matters of substance as we progressed toward a final form. They had
prepared an excellent draft, which I sought to tailor to the Mississippi legislative process. I also simplified the content for the benefit of Mississippi
legislators not well informed on the details of natural areas law.

November 18, 1977. I finished my final draft of the bill.

158

November 18 to 30, 1977. During this period, I conferred frequently with the director of the Mississippi Wildlife Heritage Committee (who represented the executive branch) and the director of the Mississippi Natural Heritage Program and continued to jawbone with Conservancy staff members to finalize the legislation for introduction.

December 1 to 15, 1977. I started talking with the members of the legislature who also served as members of the Mississippi Wildlife Heritage Committee, three senators and three representatives. These lawmakers agreed to sponsor the bill. We decided to start in the senate because one senator, a member of the heritage committee, also served as chairman of the senate Committee on Game and Fish. He assured a speedy report from his committee. This senator was also interested in being the primary sponsor because he had sponsored the act which established the heritage inventory, and he was quite proud of the heritage program. We were all happy to accommodate his wishes.

December 23, 1977. I prepared and mailed to all members of the senate Committee on Game and Fish a memorandum that contained (1) a copy of the proposed bill, (2) a synopsis and explanation of the bill, and (3) an invitation for other members of the committee to join in sponsoring the bill. I sent this out under signature of the committee chairman with a note that I had prepared the information at his request. I did not send a similar memo to the house committee chairman because I knew there would be an opportunity to explain the bill to house committee members during senate action. Incidentally, no other committee members did join as coauthors.

January 3, 1978. The bill, now called S.B. 2261, was introduced and referred to the senate Committee on Game and Fish. An amendment was added just before the bill was introduced. One section of the bill had provided that information contained in the heritage program data base would be made available to any agency or person for use in preparing environmental impact statements. Several senators feared that providing the data would "connote" state endorsement of litigation where impact statements were used as evidence in legal proceedings. The section was removed to prevent any problem that might occur in committee or on the floor. (Some members of the legislature were still sensitive over the sandhill crane litigation.) I agreed to the change because the section did not affect the specific purpose of the bill.

January 3, 1978. The bill came before the full senate for floor action and seemed destined for speedy passage when one senator raised a question regarding a tax exemption provision. The bill provided for complete *ad valorem* (the tax you pay for the privilege of owning property as opposed to "special assessment taxes for improvements or betterments") tax exemption for any property that was dedicated. The senator, concerned that large tracts would be taken from the tax rolls, asked to be allowed to amend the bill. The bill was retained in the senate while he and I worked on an amendment to provide for *pro rata* tax exemption rather than complete exemption.

January 11, 1978. The bill again came before the full senate for floor action. When the senator's tax amendment was considered, another senator raised a question about the language we used to provide the *pro rata* tax exemption. The bill was then tabled "subject to call" while we worked out suitable language to remove the second senator's objection.

January 18, 1978. The bill was conveyed to the House of Representatives.

January 20, 1978. To my surprise the bill was referred by the speaker of the house to the house Committee on Game and Fish. We had anticipated that it would be referred to the house Committee on Conservation.

During the next week, I met once or twice with the chairmen of the two committees and reached an agreement for rereferral of S.B. 2261 to the Committee on Conservation. I was relieved because I had been so sure that the bill would go to the conservation committee that I had spent no time with game and fish committee members.

January 31, 1978. The full membership of the house of representatives consented to the rereferral of S.B. 2261 to the Committee on Conservation. Ordinarily, rereferral receives no objection if both committee chairmen consent to it. (Be sure that both do consent should you need a rereferral.)

February 1 to 8, 1978. I spent a few minutes with several members of the Committee on Conservation, one at a time, to go over the legislation and answer any questions. I met with the chairman two or three times to check for problem areas and to offer assistance.

February 8, 1978. I met with the full Committee on Conservation for about 15 minutes. I explained the bill and answered one or two questions. The committee then reported the bill favorably to the full house. The chairman's active support was instrumental at this stage. He was able to indicate which members might not support the bill so that I could talk to them and try to resolve their problems.

February 11, 1978. I learned that one house member planned to offer amendments to the bill on the floor allegedly at the request of the executive branch.

I tracked down this legislator and discovered his concern. The bill authorized the Wildlife Heritage Committee to designate which agency of state government would manage each registered or dedicated site. For example, the heritage committee could designate the Forestry Commission to manage a stand of timber or the Game and Fish Commission to manage a marsh. The heritage committee could also draw up the management plan for each area, and the designated agency would have to follow it. The executive branch wished to assert—through this amendment— that the heritage committee, which consists primarily of legislators, has no constitutional authority to obligate an executive agency to manage a heritage area.

The real motive for opposition, I found out, was that the executive branch wanted to keep the management function in the Game and Fish Commission, an agency of the executive branch of government. In short, the opposition could be traced to a dispute—probably ancient—between the governor and legislature over their respective constitutional powers, and it fortunately did not mean that the executive branch opposed the protection of natural areas. Again, there is a lesson here—all disputes are not necessarily what they appear to be. You must structure the solution to meet the real problem, not the apparent problem. Still, there was a problem. I received word indirectly that unless suitable amendments were adopted, the governor might veto the bill.

Another bit of practical information: Members of the executive branch opposed the senate bill on this point as well but remained silent, apparently because they believed that the committee chairmen in the senate could muster the votes to defeat their amendments. Also, the opposition was not raised in the house until the bill reached the floor, where the executive branch apparently believed it would be able to oppose the bill most effectively. Just because no opposition appears in one house or in committee does not necessarily mean things will go smoothly in the other house or on the floor.

February 11 to 15, 1978. I worked with the dissatisfied house member and other legislators to reach a solution that would soothe the executive branch without defeating the purpose of the bill.

February 16, 1978. The bill was called up before the full house: I expected that the amendments would be offered and accepted by the committee chairman and that the bill would pass. However, once the bill was before the house, confusion arose over the amendments, and it was tabled subject to call. It turned out that the member who was to sponsor the amendments picked up the wrong amendments and did not have copies of the amendments that were agreed upon.

February 16 to 24, 1978. The amendments were changed once again because the ones agreed upon for adoption on February 16 were questioned by individuals in the executive branch.

February 24, 1978. The bill was again called before the full house and the amendments were adopted. A compromise was reached whereby the Wildlife Heritage Committee would not manage any registered or dedicated properties or draw up any management plans but would designate the agency to manage the areas to be protected. The house adopted the amendments and passed the bill.

February 27, 1978. The bill was returned to the senate with the house amendments.

March 7, 1978. The senate concurred with the house amendments to S.B. 2261.

March 23, 1978. S.B. 2261 was signed by the governor, but not without some anxious moments in the days just before he signed it. Till the very end there was some question as to whether the governor would sign the bill, even with the house amendments. At one point I was told that his natural resource advisors would not accept the amendments. I spoke to the director of the Game and Fish Commission and a gubernatorial aide for natural resources who assured me that the governor would sign the bill.

The sponsoring senator had decided to prepare to try to override a veto should the governor not sign the act. He made sure that the senate concurred with the bill in time to get the bill to the governor before the deadline for signing. Mississippi statutes provide that the governor must veto a bill within five days after he receives it from the legislature. Otherwise, it becomes law without his signature, unless he receives the bill within a certain number of days before adjournment, in which case he has time after the legislature leaves to sign or veto bills. The senator made sure that the governor received the bill in time to insure that the legislature would have an opportunity to override a veto before the session ended. Fortunately, the opportunity never arose, because with the governor's signature "The Mississippi Natural Heritage Act of 1978" (see Appendix B) became law and went into effect.

Summary

Knowledge of the legislative process and the people involved, a willingness to aid supporters, a proper foundation of education and exposure, and a continual monitoring of support and opposition will pass most bills. Each state legislator confronts thousands of bills each session. He cannot know any one bill unless its supporters take the time to educate him.

Successful lobbyists try to understand a legislator's problems, limitations, and frustrations. They are courteous, ask only for what they need, and make it easy for a legislator to support their bill.

APPENDIX A

State Legislative Sessions

Columns under **Regular sessions*** (*Legislature convenes**): Year, Month, Day, Limitation on length of session.
Columns under **Special sessions** (†*Legislature may call*): Legislature may call†, Legislature may determine subject, Limitation on length of session.

State or other jurisdiction	Year	Month	Day	Limitation on length of session (Regular)	Legislature may call†	Legislature may determine subject	Limitation on length of session (Special)
Alabama	Annual	Feb.	First Tues.(a,b)	30 L in 105 C	No	2/3 vote each house	12 L in 30 C
Alaska	Annual	Jan.	2nd Mon.(c)	None	2/3 vote of membership	Yes(e)	30 C
Arizona	Annual	Jan.	2nd Mon.	None	Petition 2/3 members, each house	Yes(e)	None
Arkansas	Odd(f)	Jan.	2nd Mon.	60 C(f)	No	(g)	None(g)
California	Even(h)	Dec.	1st Mon.	None	No	No	None
Colorado	Annual(i)	Jan.	Wed. after 1st Tues.	None	Vote 2/3 members, each house	Yes(e)	None
Connecticut	Annual(i)	Odd: Jan. Even: Feb.	Wed. after 1st Mon.	(j)	No	No	None
Delaware	Annual(d)	Jan.	2nd Tues.	June 30	Jt. call, presiding officers, both houses	Yes	None
Florida	Annual	Apr.	Tues. after 1st Mon.(b)	60 C(f)	Jt. call, presiding officers, both houses	Yes	20 C(f)
Georgia	Annual(d)	Jan.	2nd Mon.	40 L	Petition 3/5 members, each house	Yes(e)	(k)
Hawaii	Annual(d)	Jan.	3rd Wed.	60 L(f)	Petition 2/3 members, each house	Yes	30 L(f)
Idaho	Annual	Jan.	Mon. on or nearest 9th day	None	No	No	20 C
Illinois	Annual(d)	Jan.	2nd Wed.	None	Jt. call, presiding officers, both houses	Yes	None
Indiana	Annual	Jan.	2nd Mon.(b)	Odd: 61 L or Apr. 30 Even: 30 L or Mar. 15	No	Yes	30 L in 40 C
Iowa	Annual(d)	Jan.	2nd Mon.	None	Petition 2/3 members, each house	Yes	None
Kansas	Annual(d)	Jan.	2nd Mon.	Odd: none Even: 90 C(f)	Petition to governor of 2/3 members, each house	Yes	None
Kentucky	Even	Jan.	Tues. after 1st Mon.	60 L	No	No	None
Louisiana	Annual	Apr.	3rd Mon.	60 L in 85 C	Petition majority, each house	Yes(e)	30 C
Maine	Annual(i)	Jan.	1st Wed. after 1st Tues.	None	Vote of majority of each party, each house	Yes(e)	None
Maryland	Annual	Jan.	2nd Wed.	90 C(f)	Petition majority, each house	Yes	30 C
Massachusetts	Annual	Jan.	1st Wed.	None	Yes	Yes	None
Michigan	Annual(d)	Jan.	2nd Wed.	None	No	No	None
Minnesota	Odd(n)	Jan.	Tues. after 1st Mon.	120 L	No	Yes	None
Mississippi	Annual	Jan.	Tues. after 1st Mon.	(f,m)	No	No	None
Missouri	Annual	Jan.	Wed. after 1st Mon.	Odd: June 30 Even: May 15	No	No	60 C
Montana	Odd	Jan.	1st Mon.	90 L	Petition majority, each house	Yes	None
Nebraska	Annual(d)	Jan.	1st Wed. after 1st Mon.	Odd: 90 L(f) Even: 60 L(f)	Petition 2/3 members	Yes	None
Nevada	Odd	Jan.	3rd Mon.	60 C(l)	No	No	20 C(l)
New Hampshire	Odd	Jan.	1st Wed. after 1st Tues.(b)	(l)	Yes	Yes	None(l)
New Jersey	Annual(d)	Jan.	2nd Tues.	None	Petition majority, each house	Yes	None
New Mexico	Annual(i)	Jan.	3rd Tues.	Odd: 60 C Even: 30C	Petition 3/5 members, each house	Yes(e)	30 C
New York	Annual(d)	Jan.	Wed. after 1st Mon.	None	Petition 2/3 members, each house	Yes(e)	None
North Carolina	Odd(n)	Jan.	Wed. after 2nd Mon.	None	Petition 3/5 members, each house	Yes	None
North Dakota	Odd	Jan.	1st Tues. after 3rd day(b)	80 N	No	Yes	None

State	Session	Month	Convene	Limit	Special session		Limit
Ohio	Annual	Jan.	1st Mon.(n)	None	Jt. call, presiding officers, both houses	Yes	None
Oklahoma	Annual(d)	Jan.	Tues. after 1st Mon.	90 L	No	No	None
Oregon	Annual	Jan.	2nd Mon.	None	Petition majority, each house	Yes	None
Pennsylvania	Annual(d)	Jan.	1st Tues.	None	Petition majority, each house	No	None
Rhode Island	Annual(d)	Jan.	1st Tues.	60 L(l)	No	No	None
South Carolina	Annual(d)	Jan.	2nd Tues.(b)	None	No	Yes	None
South Dakota	Annual	Jan.	Odd: Tues. after 3rd Mon. / Even: Tues. after 1st Mon.	45 L / 30 L	No	No	None
Tennessee	Odd(o)	Jan.	1st Tues.(b)	90 L(l)	Petition 2/3 members, each house	Yes	30(l)
Texas	Odd	Jan.	2nd Tues.	140 C	No	No	30 C
Utah	Annual(i)	Jan.	2nd Mon.	Odd: 60 C / Even: 20 C	No	No	30 C
Vermont	Odd(o)	Jan.	Wed. after 1st Mon.	None(l)	No	Yes	None
Virginia	Annual(d)	Jan.	2nd Wed.	Odd: 30 C(f) / Even: 60 C(f)	Petition 2/3 members, each house	Yes	None
Washington	Odd	Jan.	2nd Mon.	60 C	No	Yes	None
West Virginia	Annual	Jan.	2nd Wed.(p)	60 C(f,q)	Petition 3/5 members, each house	Yes(r)	None
Wisconsin	Annual	Jan.	1st Tues. after Jan. 8(s)	None	No	No	None
Wyoming	Annual(i)	Jan. / Feb.	Odd: 2nd Tues. / Even: 2nd Tues.	40 L / 20 L	No	Yes	None
American Samoa	Annual	July	2nd Mon.	30 L	No	No	None
Guam	Annual(d)	Jan.	2nd Mon.	Apr. 30(f)	No	No	None
Puerto Rico	Annual(d)	Jan.	2nd Mon.	50 C	No	No	20
Virgin Islands	Annual(d)	Jan.	2nd Mon.	75 L	No	No	None

Key: L Legislative day C Calendar day N Natural day

* All states elect new legislatures in November of even-numbered years except Kentucky, Louisiana, Mississippi, New Jersey, and Virginia. Alabama, Louisiana, Maryland, and Mississippi elect all legislators at the same time to four-year terms (see the table on pages 238 and 239).

† The following states provide for a special session to only consider bills vetoed after adjournment sine die: Connecticut, Hawaii, Louisiana, Missouri (even years only), and Washington.

(a) During the quadrennial election year, sessions convene on the 2nd Tues. in Jan.

(b) Legislature meets in organizational session. Alabama: second Tuesday in January after quadrennial election; Florida: 14th day following each general election; Indiana: third Tuesday after first Monday in November for one day only; New Hampshire: first Wednesday of December, even-numbered years; North Dakota: December following general election to reconvene at a time prescribed by law, but no later than January 8; South Carolina: first Tuesday after certification of the election of its members for no more than 3 days; Tennessee: first Tuesday in January for no more than 15 C days to organize and introduce bills, reconvenes on fourth Tuesday in February.

(c) Except in the January immediately following the quadrennial general election, the first regular session will convene on the third Monday in January.

(d) The legislature meets in two annual sessions, each adjourning sine die. Bills carry over from first to second session.

(e) Only if legislature convenes itself. Special sessions called by the legislature are unlimited in scope in Arizona, Georgia, Maine, and New Mexico.

(f) Session may be extended for an indefinite period of time by vote of members in both houses. Arkansas: 2/3 vote (this extension can permit the legislature to meet in even years); Florida: 3/5 vote; Hawaii: petition of 2/3 membership for not more than 15 days; Kansas: 2/3 vote of those elected members; Maryland: 3/5 vote for 30 additional days; Mississippi: 2/3 vote of those present may extend for 30 C days, no limit on extensions; Nebraska: 4/5 vote; Virginia: 2/3 vote for up to 30 days; West Virginia: 2/3 vote(s) in the governor's call, it may by a 2/3 vote of the members of both houses take up subject(s) of its own choosing in a session of up to 15 days.

(g) After the legislature has disposed of the subject(s) of the subject(s) of its own choosing in a session of up to 15 days.

(j) Odd years: not later than first Wednesday after first Monday in June; even years: not later than first Wednesday after first Monday in May.

(k) Limited to 70 days if called by governor and 30 days if called at petition of legislature, except for impeachment proceedings.

(l) Indirect restrictions only since legislator's pay, per diem, or daily allowance stops, but session may continue. Nevada: no limit on allowances. New Hampshire: constitutional limit on expenses.

(h) Regular sessions commence on the first Monday in December of each even-numbered year (following the general election) and continue until November 30 of the next even-numbered year. It may recess from time to time, and may be recalled into regular session.

(i) Second session of legislature is basically limited to budget and fiscal matters. Maine: In addition, legislation in the governor's call, study committee legislation, and initiated measures. New Mexico: legislature may consider bills vetoed by the governor or at the preceding session. Utah: legislature may consider nonbudget matters after 2/3 vote of each house. New Mexico: legislature may consider measures for special sessions; Tennessee: constitutional limit on per diem and travel allowance only, excluding organizational session.

(m) The first session of a new legislature, every other even year at the beginning of the gubernatorial term, is limited to 125 C days; other years 90 C days.

(n) First Monday in January or the day after if the first Monday falls on a legal holiday.

(p) The legislature may and in practice has divided the session to meet in even years also. Following each gubernatorial election, the legislature convenes on the second Wednesday of January to organize, but recesses until the second Wednesday in February for the start of the 60-day session.

(q) Governor must extend until the general appropriation is passed.

(t) According to a 1955 attorney general's opinion, when the legislature has petitioned to the governor to be called into session, it may then act on any matter.

(s) The legislature by joint resolution establishes the calendar dates of session activity for the remainder of the biennium at the beginning of the odd-numbered year. These dates may be subject to change.

APPENDIX B

Mississippi Natural Heritage Act of 1978

49-5-141. Short title.

Sections 49-5-141 to 49-5-157 shall be known and may be cited as the "Mississippi Natural Heritage Law of 1978."

SOURCES: Laws, 1978, ch. 415, §1, eff from and after passage (approved March 23, 1978).

49-5-143. Legislative findings and declaration.

(1) The legislature finds and declares that there is a need for additional organized, accessible information to identify and make known the types and locations of plant and animal life, geological areas and other natural areas in this state.

(2) The legislature further finds and declares that a system of protection and management of these areas should be implemented and maintained through a procedure of voluntary action by the owners of the property on which these areas may be located.

SOURCES: Laws, 1978, ch. 415, §2, eff from and after passage (approved March 23, 1978).

49-5-145. Purpose.

(1) The legislature states that the purpose of sections 49-5-141 to 49-5-157 is to establish a registration procedure by which owners of natural areas may voluntarily agree to manage and protect the areas according to rules set forth by the Mississippi Wildlife Heritage Committee.

(2) The legislature states that the purpose of sections 49-5-141 to 49-5-157 is also to establish a dedication procedure by which owners of natural areas may voluntarily agree to convey any or all of their right, title and interest in the property to the State of Mississippi to be managed and protected by an appropriate agency designated by the Wildlife Heritage Committee for the people of Mississippi.

SOURCES: Laws, 1978, ch. 415, §3, eff from and after passage (approved March 23, 1978).

Cross references—

As to creation, membership, and meetings of the Wildlife Heritage Committee, see §§49-5-61 et seq.

49-5-147. Definitions.

For the purposes of sections 49-5-141 to 49-5-157, the following words shall have the meaning ascribed herein unless the context shall otherwise require:

(a) "Committee" shall mean the Mississippi Wildlife Heritage Committee.

(b) "Natural area" shall mean an area of land, water or air, or combination thereof, which contains an element of the state's natural diversity, including, but not limited to, individual plant or animal life, natural geological areas, habitats of endangered or threatened species, ecosystems or any other area of unique ecological, scientific or educational interest.

(c) "Register" shall mean the act of agreement between the owner of a natural area and the committee for designation of the natural area and for its placement

166

on the register of natural areas by voluntary agreement between the owner of the natural area and the committee.

(d) "Register of natural areas" shall mean a listing of natural areas which are being managed by the owner of the natural area according to the rules and regulations of the committee.

(e) "Natural area preserve" shall mean a natural area which is voluntarily dedicated.

(f) "Dedicate" shall mean the transfer to the committee of any estate, interest or right in any natural area to be held for the people of Mississippi in a manner provided in section 49-5-155.

SOURCES: Laws, 1978, ch. 415, §4, eff from and after passage (approved March 23, 1978).
Cross references—
As to creation, membership, and meetings of the Wildlife Heritage Committee, see §§49-5-61 et seq.

49-5-149. Powers and duties of committee.

The committee shall have the following powers and duties:

(a) to utilize inventory data compiled by the Mississippi Wildlife Heritage Program concerning the natural areas of the state;

(b) to accept on behalf of the people of Mississippi any right, title or interest to any natural area;

(c) to establish and maintain a register of natural areas;

(d) to select natural areas for placement on the register of natural areas or for dedication as a natural area preserve, or both;

(e) to provide for the management of natural area preserves by designating an appropriate agency to manage the preserve in accordance with the provisions set forth in the articles of dedication which establish the natural area as a natural area preserve.

(f) to cooperate with any agency of the United States, the State of Mississippi and any other state, any political subdivision of this state and with private persons or organizations to implement the provisions of sections 49-5-141 to 49-5-157;

(g) to discharge any other duty or action necessary to implement the provisions of sections 49-5-141 to 49-5-157.

SOURCES: Laws, 1978, ch. 415, §5, eff from and after passage (approved March 23, 1978).
Cross references—
As to creation, membership, and meetings of the Wildlife Heritage Committee, see §§49-5-61 et seq.

49-5-151. Register of natural areas.

The committee shall publish and revise at least annually a register of natural areas using the inventory of natural areas compiled by the Mississippi Wildlife Heritage Program.

SOURCES: Laws, 1978, ch. 415, §6, eff from and after passage (approved March 23, 1978).

Cross references—

As to creation, membership and meetings of the Wildlife Heritage Committee, see §§49-5-61 et seq.

49-5-153. Registration of natural areas.

(1) The owner of any natural area on the registry may, if the committee so agrees, register the natural area by executing a voluntary agreement with the committee for the owner to manage and protect the natural area according to the rules and regulations promulgated by the committee and to give the committee first option to purchase the natural area. If the owner agrees to register the area, he shall be given a certificate of registration and shall be committed to manage the area according to the terms of the agreement with the committee. The agreement may be terminated by either party after thirty (30) days written notice. The owner, upon termination, shall surrender the certificate; provided, however, the first option to purchase shall remain with the committee unless the committee shall relinquish the option in writing.

(2) Any property acquired by the committee or any other agency of the state or political subdivision thereof pursuant to any other authority in law may be registered according to the provisions of this section.

SOURCES: Laws, 1978, ch. 415, §7, eff from and after passage (approved March 23, 1978).

Cross references—

As to creation, membership and meetings of the Wildlife Heritage Committee, see §§ 49-5-61 et seq.

49-5-155. Dedication of natural areas to committee—exemption from ad valorem taxation.

(1) The owner of any natural area may dedicate that area as a natural area preserve by executing with the committee articles of dedication. The articles shall transfer such portion of the owner's estate as agreed upon by the owner and the committee to the committee for the people of Mississippi.

(2) The committee may acquire articles of dedication for consideration or by donation, devise or bequest. The articles of dedication shall be recorded in the office of the chancery clerk of the county in which any or all of the natural area is located before the area shall become a natural area preserve.

(3) The committee may dedicate any property owned by the committee as natural area preserve by filing and recording articles of dedication in the office of the chancery clerk of the county in which any or all of the area is located.

(4) The articles of dedication shall contain:

(a) provisions for the management, custody and use of the natural area preserve;

(b) provisions which define the rights and privileges of the owner and the committee of the managing agency; and

(c) such other provisions as the owner or committee shall deem necessary to discharge the provisions of sections 49-5-141 to 49-5-157 or to complete the transfer.

(5) The committee shall agree to no articles of dedication which do not provide for the protection, preservation and management of the natural area in a manner consistent with the intent and purposes of sections 49-5-141 to 49-5-157.

(6) Any interest in real property owned by the committee in a natural area preserve shall be exempt from all ad valorem taxation levied by the State of Mississippi or any county or municipality or other political subdivision of this state. Any person who shall convey any interest in real property to the committee for the purposes set forth in sections 49-5-141 to 49-5-157 shall be entitled to have the assessment of such property reduced by the amount of the value of the interest conveyed to the committee. The authorities responsible for determining and making the assessment shall also determine the value of the interest conveyed to the committee. This reduction in the assessment of such property shall terminate when the interest conveyed to the committee terminates.

(7) The committee shall be the agency of the State of Mississippi primarily responsible for acquisition of natural area preserves, but no provision of sections 49-5-141 to 49-5-157 shall be construed to limit the committee's authority to acquire other property. Any property acquired by the committee or any other agency of the state or political subdivision thereof pursuant to any other authority in law may be dedicated according to the provisions of this section.

(8) No provisions of sections 49-5-141 to 49-5-157 shall be construed to limit the authority of any other agency to acquire and dedicate natural areas according to the provisions of sections 49-5-141 to 49-5-157.

SOURCES: Laws, 1978, ch. 415, §8, eff from and after passage (approved March 23, 1978).

Cross references—

As to creation, membership and meetings of the Wildlife Heritage Committee, see §§49-5-61 et seq.

49-5-157. Management, protection and inspection of natural area preserves.

A natural area preserve is held in trust by the State of Mississippi for present and future generations and shall be managed and protected according to the rules and regulations set forth by the committee. A natural area preserve is hereby declared to be at the highest, best and most important use for the public.

(2) The committee shall inspect or provide for the inspection of at least annually, each natural area preserve to insure that the terms of the articles of dedication are being respected.

SOURCES: Laws, 1978, ch. 415, §9, eff from and after passage (approved March 23, 1978).

Cross references—

As to creation, membership and meetings of the Wildlife Heritage Committee, see §§49-5-61 et seq.

CHAPTER THIRTEEN

ENVIRONMENTAL REVIEW

So far these chapters have considered mainly ways to protect natural diversity by negotiating with landowners. We've arrived at the landowner's doorstep offering information, recognition, cash, tax savings, and management advice. However, a thorough state program to protect natural diversity must also be able to inform prospective developers—both private and public—whenever they plan a project that would threaten an element of natural diversity.

This information must reach developers routinely, before they have committed themselves psychologically or financially to their ideas. Experience has demonstrated that public agencies and private developers alike will adjust their plans to avoid environmental impacts if they are convinced that there is a good reason to do so, if they haven't already invested too much, and if the profitability of a project does not depend on a precise location.

Their attitude makes sense. Few people would choose to destroy something commonly valued if they didn't feel they had to. More directly, early warnings of potential conflicts can avoid hearings and litigation, potentially saving a developer millions of dollars and years of delay.

Major Environmental Review Programs

Many laws and programs have been established to cushion the impact upon the natural environment caused by the expansion of human enterprise. The best known and most influential is the National Environmental Policy Act (NEPA), which requires the production of environmental impact statements whenever a major federal action or state action funded by federal money would significantly affect the quality of the human environment. NEPA has spawned "little NEPAs" in 15 states (see Table 1), and has also led most federal agencies to analyze in writing the potential environmental impact of resource planning actions.

Other laws have established programs that regulate development within potentially fragile areas, such as coastal zones, areas supporting habitat for endangered species, wild and scenic river corridors, floodplains, or coal-laden areas deemed unsuitable for mining. Still others at least re-

171

quire a critical examination of all projects requiring certain kinds of permits or licences (see Table 1).

The Need for Information

All of these programs have, or should have, one thing in common — they all depend on information. Decisionmakers simply have to know which portions of the landscape are significant, and, of those, which are most significant.

A transportation department considering several alternative routes for a highway needs comparative information about the phenomena found along each route on which to base its decision. Once a decision has been made and the department has applied for permits or licences, authorities must likewise be able to scrutinize the area selected in order to decide whether or not to give a green light. Thus, at both stages — planning and environmental review — officials need to know whether there are significant natural elements that could be damaged by proposed activities.

State natural heritage programs — which so far have been discussed only in light of their ability to indicate protection priorities — are also designed to provide mapped comparative ecological data to project sponsors and public officials. Each heritage program gathers and manages information on endangered species of plants and animals as well as the plant communities and natural aquatic systems represented in each state. (The organization of a heritage program is discussed more thoroughly in Chapter Two.)

Most of the 23 states, which, as of March 1980, have installed heritage data base systems, have used this mapped, locational information extensively, both to focus their environmental review programs and for guidance in resource planning. Major industries have also perceived the advantages of an ecological data base, and in some states have supported heritage programs financially. For example, the Indiana heritage program was half-funded initially by a consortium of five publicly owned utility companies. At a ceremony marking the establishment of the Indiana heritage program, the president of one of those companies remarked:

> As one of the five electric companies supporting the Indiana heritage programs we feel an obligation to consider the environmental effects of the projects we undertake. A lack of centralized information about wildlife and the unique natural areas in the state have

Table 1—A Sample

	Approved Coastal Zone Management Programs[1]	Little NEPAs[2] Statutory	Little NEPAs[2] Administrative	State Endangered Plant Species Law[3]	Cooperative Agreements with the Office of Endangered Species[4] Animals	Plants
Alabama	X			X		
Alaska	X					
Arizona					X	
Arkansas					X	
California	X	X		X	X	X
Colorado		X			X	
Connecticut		X			X	X
Delaware	X				X	
Florida				X	X	
Georgia				X	X	
Hawaii	X	X		X	X	
Idaho				X	X	
Illinois				X	X	
Indiana		X				
Iowa				X	X	
Kansas					X	
Kentucky						
Louisiana				X		
Maine	X				X	
Maryland	X	X		X	X	
Massachusetts	X	X			X	
Michigan	X		X	X	X	X
Minnesota		X			X	
Mississippi						
Missouri					X	
Montana		X			X	
Nebraska				X	X	
Nevada				X	X	
New Hampshire					X	
New Jersey	X		X		X	
New Mexico				X	X	
New York		X		X	X	
North Carolina	X	X		X	X	
North Dakota						
Ohio				X		
Oklahoma						
Oregon	X			X		
Pennsylvania					X	
Rhode Island	X			X		
South Carolina	X				X	
South Dakota		X			X	
Tennessee					X	
Texas			X			
Utah			X		X	
Vermont				X		
Virginia		X		X	X	
Washington	X	X			X	X
West Virginia						
Wisconsin	X	X		X	X	
Wyoming						

hampered our attempt to consider these environmental aspects in the past. We feel the heritage program will provide us—and anyone else—with the input we need to give special consideration to these areas and preserve them for posterity.[5]

Heritage Programs and the A-95 Review Process

A heritage data base is most useful when it can be consulted routinely, whenever someone desires to alter a state's landscape significantly. The A-95 review process offers a good example of how heritage data can help any state comment intelligently on the ecological impacts of proposed projects.

In 1976 the Federal Office of Management and Budget (OMB) issued Circular A-95, requiring all potential project developers needing federal permits, grants, or licences in order to proceed with their plans (this includes almost all major projects) to: (1) describe their proposal in writing and (2) to circulate the description among all state agencies that might have relevant knowledge of environmental impacts. OMB also insisted that each state establish a "clearinghouse" to serve as a distribution center for all the project descriptions that were to come. Thus, each state clearinghouse, which in most states has turned out to be a clerk or two, was to receive the blizzard of paper, distribute project descriptions among appropriate state agencies, receive the return comments of each agency, and rerefer them to the permitting authority or the applicant.

Almost all of the project descriptions reach a major natural resources agency, and once there, they trickle down to a person who coordinates A-95 responses on behalf of the department. Without the ability to compare a map of the proposed project site against a map of the same area which locates the ecological elements of concern in the vicinity, and without the ability to consult files that reveal just *how* rare, endangered, or otherwise significant those occurrences are, that coordinator's ability to help the department respond meaningfully is greatly diminished. In Indiana and Tennessee the heritage program coordinates the A-95 review responses for the entire Department of Natural Resources. The Tennessee heritage program in 1979 reviewed over 2,500 descriptions. Below is a case example of how heritage data can assist the A-95 review process.

Water Lines and Cedar Glades: A Tennessee Example

In 1964 Dr. Elsie Quarterman, a professor of botany at Vanderbilt Uni-

174

versity in Nashville, Tennessee, spent part of the spring helping one of her Ph.D. students locate permanent sampling plots for fieldwork relating to his dissertation on *Psoralea subacaulis*, a plant species endemic (restricted) to the cedar glades of central Tennessee. During that summer they discovered several healthy populations of *Psoralea*, and also of several other cedar glade endemic plant species.

At one of the sites they visited in Marshall County not far from the Duck River, they found populations of at least three cedar glade endemics. They collected a sample of each for the Vanderbilt herbarium and entered a specimen sample into the herbarium on April 25, 1964.

Eleven years later in April 1975, the Tennessee Department of Conservation signed a contract with The Nature Conservancy, establishing the Tennessee Natural Heritage Program. After the staff was selected and hired, they consulted the scientific community in Tennessee to determine which plant and animal species were important enough to monitor through data and to establish a plant community classification system. By the fall of 1976 a committee of five distinguished Tennessee taxonomists had completed a list of the rare vascular flora of Tennessee.[6]

The heritage program staff adopted that list as the list of plants for which they would keep data and began to collect information on the status, rarity, distribution, location, and condition of known occurrences of each plant species on the list. Included among the "special plants" were *Psoralea subacaulis* and the other two species Dr. Quarterman and her doctoral student collected in Marshall County in 1964.

Heritage researchers, seeking historical records for the plants on their list at the major herbaria of Tennessee, found their way to the Vanderbilt herbarium in March 1977. During their visit, they recorded the information Dr. Quarterman had entered with the plant specimens from Marshall County 13 years earlier. When they returned to the heritage office, the workers mapped the location of the Marshall County occurrences on the Verona 64 S.E. 7½-minute U.S. Geological Survey quadrangle map and entered relevant information about the plants at the site into both manual and computer files.

From the beginning Tennessee conservation officials had been especially interested in the heritage program's potential for handling a tide of environmental review requests. The program staff had been assigned to the Division of Planning, and as soon as enough data were available, a heritage staff member was assigned the task of reviewing the hundreds of environmental review requests, including A-95 descriptions that reached the department each month.

On January 15, 1980, the heritage program's environmental review coordinator received a standard A-95 review document describing the Marshall County government's desire to apply for a $500,000 grant from the federal Department of Housing and Urban Development (HUD). The grant was to be used to finance the extension of water lines further into rural areas of Marshall County. As usual, a map of the proposed extension routes was attached.

The heritage worker walked over to the map file, pulled the Verona 64 S.E. 7½-minute quadrangle map and examined it. One of the proposed extension routes appeared to run through a cedar glade, containing populations of several endemic plants, some of which because of their extremely restricted range were now beginning to receive attention as being of national significance. The worker consulted the occurrence files and found the information Dr. Quarterman had entered 16 years earlier while helping her student research *Psoralea subacaulis,* as well as a good body of subsequent information about still other occurrences at the site. The plants appeared rare, restricted, and healthy at the site.

To make certain, the Tennessee heritage staff botanist conferred with a botanist employed by the Tennessee Valley Authority's Heritage Program (the only regional heritage program) who had conducted recent fieldwork in the area on cedar glade endemic plants. The TVA botanist confirmed that the plants were still viable at the site and that they had been mapped correctly. The two botanists agreed that the water line could probably be installed without destroying the plants, if it were placed along the opposite side of a nearby road.

On the basis of this information, the Tennessee Department of Conservation recommended to the state's A-95 clearinghouse that one of the water pipelines proposed for Marshall County be shifted from the south to the north side of the road.

A Marshall County judge was the official in charge of submitting the waterline proposal to HUD. When he received the comments from the state clearinghouse—including the adjustment recommended by the Department of Conservation—he promptly wrote a letter to HUD's regional office in Knoxville, stating that the county wished to amend its preapplication for a community block grant funding by shifting one pipeline route in order to avoid a group of rare plants. At this writing the application is still pending.

The conservation department's recommendation was specific, based on reliable and recent information, and was offered as part of a systematic process before HUD funds were committed to the water lines. Most important, the recommendation did not ask the county to cancel its plans but merely to adjust one of their lines to avoid a significant component of Tennessee's natural heritage—something the county could do without much trouble since no pipe had been laid. This case shows that heritage data, provided at the right time and as part of a well-organized system, can lead to sensible adjustments, which can protect the natural landscape without controversy or litigation. In this instance the process, because it was well organized, was able to synthesize the work of scores of people over 16 years—from Dr. Quarterman to the Marshall County judge (few of whom knew each other) in order to protect something truly precious.

A Range of Environmental Review Responses

Not all heritage recommendations lead to project adjustments. The programs have decided not to comment unless data give them something specific to say, and then generally only to point out possible points of conflict and the importance of the natural elements at stake—in terms of their known rarity, distribution, and condition.

Usually, when heritage data indicates no apparent conflict in reviewing an application, the program staff says just that. The staff does not, and cannot, certify that an element is not present at a given site simply because there are no occurrence records. As one sage put it, "absence of evidence is not evidence of absence." If there are no occurrences of natural elements within the vicinity of a proposed site, but a sponsor has applied to place a project within a habitat-type likely to contain occurrences of significant elements, the program staff usually recommends that the area be surveyed.

In several instances the program staff has stated that data do not support the designation of a critical area. For example, in 1979 the U.S. Department of the Interior requested that the Minnesota Department of Natural Resources (MDNR) consider registering two of its holdings as National Natural Landmarks. MDNR officials asked the Minnesota Natural

177

Heritage Program staff to review these proposals and recommend a course of action. The program was able to evaluate the sites very specifically, as this excerpt from the heritage recommendation shows.

If the Jay Cooke stand is proposed as one of several representatives of the northern hardwood type, we cannot understand why it was proposed and the Magney Park site deactivated (for landmark consideration). Canopy data for the two sites (Flaccus and Ohmann, 1964) indicate comparable relative importance of dominant canopy species, comparable virgin status, and equal numbers of canopy species at the two sites. Independent data in the heritage data system indicate the presence of at least one potential element (*Panax trifolium* L.) at the Magney site. Verification of a second potential element (*Actaea pachypoda* Ell.) is pending. Sampling of a 400-square-meter area in the Magney site during the summer of 1979 generated a list of 16 herbaceous species, including five of those listed by Stearns (1951) as typical of northern hardwood stands. This is the same number of typical species as on the list included in the on-site evaluation for the Jay Cooke site.

Heritage Data and Planning

Heritage data have important implications beyond environmental review. Many of the well-established programs have secured contracts to provide locational information for planning agencies, such as the federal Office of Surface Mining, which in several coal states has used heritage data to help determine areas unsuitable for mining. In Wyoming, heritage data on fish have been used to develop a stream quality classification system. In one instance heritage data are being used to help plan a course of action in the event of an environmental emergency. The Rhode Island Heritage Program and the Rhode Island Coastal Resources Center are together developing an "oil spill contingency manual" to be used by state workers in preventing and cleaning up oil spills. The heritage program staff has contributed by analyzing its data to compile an inventory of significant natural areas on the Rhode Island coast for the Department of Environmental Management (DEM), the agency responsible for dealing with oil spills. DEM has then devised specific strategies for protecting each area against spills.

Summary

This chapter has considered several ways in which mapped locational data on the elements of a state's natural ecological diversity can be used to protect the places where they occur. Conflicts are usually based on misunderstanding—too little information too late. Data provided by state heritage programs can reach project sponsors before commitments to projects are made.

CHAPTER FOURTEEN

BUILDING AN ARK

Suppose we attempt to model the tools described in the previous chapters to preserve what remains of natural ecological diversity in an "average" state. Of course, there is no such thing as an average state, and if there were, no resident would admit that he lived in it. (One well-traveled conservationist says that no matter where he is, officials tell him their state is (1) the most politically conservative state in the Union, (2) the hardest state in which to get anything done, and (3) the biological crossroads of America.)

Still, by considering the physical, economic, legal, and institutional resources present in the various states, it is possible to stitch together a composite state called "Transylvania," recognizable to no one but useful for laboratory purposes.

Transylvania Revealed

Following is a rough description of Transylvania, revealed in terms of its physical landscape, human use, and ownership.

PHYSICAL FEATURES
Acreage - 46,000,000
Physiography - six distinctive ecoregions, including foothills,
        mountains, grasslands, coastal, forest, till plain.

LAND USE	Percent
Cropland	18
Pasture and range	30
Forest land	33
Urban	2
Transport	1
Farmsteads	0.5
Rural parks	8
Wildlife	0.25
Defense	7
Institutional	0.25
Total	100.00

LAND OWNERSHIP
Federally owned - 15,300,000 acres

a) Bureau of Land Management - 9,513,000 acres
b) U.S. Forest Service   - 3,709,500 acres
c) U.S. Fish and Wildlife Service - 607,142 acres
d) National Park Service   - 505,951 acres
e) Other   - 964,407 acres

Natural Diversity in Transylvania

The Transylvania State Natural Heritage Program, a division of the Transylvania Department of Natural Resources, was established four years ago. During the first two years, staff workers collected data on occurrences of natural elements mainly from secondary sources, such as herbaria, literature references, museums, and conversations with scientific experts. Having exhausted many secondary sources, and aware of the portions within the state about which too little was known, the staff, assisted by scientists working within other state agencies, conducted a series of intensive field surveys, collecting considerable new information.

Last autumn, after summer fieldwork had been completed and new data had been entered into manual and computer files, heritage workers analyzed the data base in an attempt to determine the status of natural diversity in Transylvania at that moment. Following is an account of their effort.

Plant Communities. The heritage program has adopted a system that classifies the vegetation of Transylvania into 90 distinctive plant communities (such as a beech-maple forest or a blue-gramma dominated prairie). The heritage staff sought first to determine the status, or overall well-being of each community type, then to determine which plant community types were in greatest need of conservation.

They next sought to identify places where healthy, viable examples of, first, the priority communities (those in greatest need) and, then, the rest could be protected. In organizing their efforts, they produced element status summary sheets for each element (see Table 1, Chapter 3). They came up with the following:

Elements—Plant Communities

Total number of plant community types	90
Number of elements occurring at least twice on protected land*	24

*For purposes of this discussion, a protected area is a place managed deliberately to perpetuate an element of natural diversity.

Number of elements requiring further attention	66
Distribution:	
a. Number of community types endemic to state	5
b. Number of community types restricted to one multistate biogeographic region, and rare throughout range	3
Rarity: Number of community types having three or fewer occurrences in state, not included above as having restricted distribution	10
Endangerment status: Number of community types known to be in serious decline, regardless of whether they happen to be rare or restricted at time of data analysis	5
Appropriateness of land conservation: Number of community types included above which could not be benefited through land conservation	0
Priority elements	23

Element Occurrences—Plant Communities. The heritage staff searched the element status summaries to help them find the best places to protect, first, the 23 priority elements, and, then, the remaining 43 unprotected elements. In screening the data for sites, they asked:

1. Can a viable occurrence of the element be protected here?
2. Can the occurrence be defended, immediately and indefinitely, at this place?
3. Are there occurrences of any other elements within or near the community here?
4. Is this an excellent example, or the best we have in Transylvania, of this element?

For seven of the most endangered priority elements, the staff decided to identify two sites as priorities, thus the staff identified the following occurrences.

Occurrences of priorities (two different sites were chosen for seven especially vulnerable elements)	30 sites
Occurrences of other unprotected community types	43 sites
Total	73 sites

Aquatic Systems. They applied the same process of analysis to the 30 aquatic systems (such as a bog or oxbow lake) that scientists had identified as distinctive and characteristic of Transylvania. They obtained the following results.

Elements

Total number of aquatic element types	30
Number of elements occurring at least twice on protected land	7

Number of elements requiring further attention   23
Distribution:
a. Endemic to Transylvania   4
b. Restricted to one biogeographic province, and rare   3
Rarity: Other elements with three or fewer occurrences   3
Endangerment status: Elements in serious decline, regardless of rarity
or distribution   1
Appropriateness of land conservation: Number of elements which
could not benefit from land conservation   <u>1*</u>
Priority elements   10

Element Occurrences. Asking the same questions they asked of the various plant community elements, and again identifying two places for the most endangered types, the staff identified the following occurrences.

Occurrences of priorities   12 sites
Occurrences of other unprotected aquatic systems   <u>13 sites</u>
Total   25 sites

Special Plants and Special Animals. The staff next considered plant and animal species. It was somewhat easier to consider the distribution and endangerment status of species than communities since the Federal Endangered Species Act of 1973 has promoted the examination of some species in terms of their national distribution.

When they considered element occurrences, they found that some species could best be protected at places already identified as the best sites for plant communities or aquatic systems. They also found that rather frequently more than one species could be protected at the same place, and sometimes at a good plant community site. They adjusted their computations accordingly.

ELEMENTS	PLANTS	ANIMALS
Total number	200	100
Protected adequately	<u>50</u>	<u>30</u>
Requiring further attention	150	70
Of those requiring further attention:		
Restricted	10	8
Rare but not restricted	7	5
Otherwise endangered	<u>3</u>	<u>3</u>
Subtotal	20	16

*An extensive system of saltwater marshes is protected adequately through a strong coastal zone statute and statewide plan of implementation but is becoming contaminated through industrial pollution.

Not needing land conservation	0	2
Priority elements	20	14

Element Occurrences (considering places where more than one element can be protected).

For priorities	15 sites	12 sites
Other unprotected elements	80 sites	30 sites
Total sites	95	42

Totals for All Four Element Classes

ELEMENT CLASS	NUMBER OF SITES CONTAINING PRIORITIES	SITES CONTAINING OCCURRENCES OF OTHER UNPROTECTED ELEMENTS	TOTAL
Plant communities	30	43	73
Aquatic systems	12	13	25
Plant species	15	80	95
Animal species	12	30	42
Total	69	166	235

Thus, the staff had determined that an adequate sample of at least the rarest, best representative, and most endangered elements of Transylvania's natural diversity could be protected at 235 places, and that 69 of them needed help quickly. It took some time for a coalition of scientists, professional conservationists, and volunteers to design potential preserves at these places, applying the process of analysis described in Chapter Three, page 20, "Factors in Preserve Design." Perhaps the most noxious chore was the investigation of ownership, wrought from many afternoons of diligence at Transylvania's county courthouses.

When the dust had cleared, they discovered that the 69 priority sites contained 150 tracts (100 privately owned) and that the remaining 166 sites contained 500 tracts (300 privately owned). The pattern of ownership, to the extent one existed, was amazing. The overall ratio of private/public ownership approximated that of the state as a whole (60 percent/40 percent), but some sites were owned by a welter of agencies, corporations (50 large corporations turned out to own 30 percent of all private land in the state), absentee owners, and residents.

Carrying matters a bit further, they assumed all private land was for sale and tried to calculate the cost of purchasing all the land required to protect Transylvania's ecological heritage. The price tag, computed as follows, was staggering and discouraging.

	PRIORITY	OTHER	TOTAL
Total private acreage desired (average 1,000 acres/site, 60 percent privately owned)	41,400 acres	99,600	141,000
Cost of wetland (50 percent of all acreage, at $500/acre average)	$10,350,000	$49,800,000	$ 60,150,000
Cost of upland (50 percent of all acreage, at $1,000/acre average)	$20,700,000	$99,600,000	$120,300,000
Total purchase price	$31,050,000	$149,400,000	$180,450,000

"A hundred and eighty million dollars!" the staff exclaimed in unison. "Even Missouri couldn't handle that," said the staff zoologist, acquainted with Missouri's ⅛-cent sales tax for land acquisition. But after a despondent period, they decided to inventory the resources available to protect the places they had identified, just as they had helped to inventory the landscape itself. They knew they would need money, laws, and people who shared their interest. They discovered the following assets.

Human Resources Available for Protecting Transylvania's Natural Diversity

1. The five-person heritage staff.
2. Six divisions within the Department of Natural Resources.
3. The Nature Conservancy, Transylvania State Office, three professional staff people. The Nature Conservancy, Transylvania Chapter, 1,000 members.
4. Three local land trusts.
5. Ten other conservation groups, total staff of 30, membership 5,000.
6. Three national forests, with professional scientists on staff.
7. Three national parks, with professional scientists.
8. Seven national wildlife refuges, with professional scientists.
9. Ten soil conservation service offices, ten extension agents.
10. Sixty county ASCS offices.
11. A regional representative of the Research Natural Area Committee.
12. Three major state universities.

13. Fourteen colleges.
14. Seven junior colleges.
15. Six in-state, land-related research groups.

Laws and Regulations and Promising Arrangements

1. A Nature Preserves Act, providing for dedication and registration of natural areas.
2. A good conservation easement statute.
3. A Transylvania Endangered Species Act.
4. A cooperative agreement with the federal Office of Endangered Species.
5. The Transylvania Heritage Program coordinated with the Department of Natural Resources' Environmental Review Program.
6. A state NEPA.
7. A good coastal zone statute.

Potential Financial Resources

1. The department was allocated $1.5 million to acquire land for outdoor recreation.
2. The general public might be willing to support a well-conceived program to protect its ecological heritage, through numerous means.
3. The Land and Water Conservation Fund, applied as appropriate.
4. The ability of The Nature Conservancy to purchase property at reduced prices (29 percent of all Transylvania taxpayers took charitable deductions in 1980).
5. Six major foundations, with combined assets of $10 million and a broad range of giving purposes intended mainly to promote the well-being of Transylvanians.
6. Eleven minor foundations, with combined assets of $1 million.
7. Forty large national corporations with property in Transylvania.
8. Five hundred corporations with annual sales exceeding $1 million.

Awareness of all this potential brightened their spirits tremendously. The heritage staff discussed with DNR officials the idea of attempting to organize a "protection planning council," at first consisting of a small working group, representatives of resources, agencies, and private conservation groups to consider a broad effort to protect the areas in question.

187

They were aware of a good precedent for collective action in Tennessee, where a group that calls itself "The Tennessee Protection Planning Committee" has met regularly since late 1979 to consider how its members can work together to protect a group of natural areas that have been identified mainly by the Tennessee Heritage Program. State, federal, and private members of the committee together pursue common conservation goals. Two members, the Tennessee Wildlife Resources Agency and the Tennessee Department of Conservation, were designated by the state as the agencies responsible for protecting Tennessee's native plants and animals. The representative from the U.S. Fish and Wildlife Service has expressed his agency's interest in protecting large areas containing whole ecosystems. The Tennessee office of The Nature Conservancy is interested both in sites providing habitat for rare and endangered species and in protecting communities and natural systems. The participants discuss specific sites and consider protection strategies. Each organization is able to acquire land, but because each is limited in a somewhat different way, all groups can benefit from collaboration with the others.

The Transylvania Protection Planning Council was established in short order. The group in turn established, through funding provided by a private foundation,* a Transylvania landowner contact program. By the end of a year program representatives had met most of the owners of 400 privately owned property tracts within the sites identified by the heritage program. The representatives brought back a harvest of useful information, tabulated roughly as follows:

Private Ownership of
Tracts Within Identified Areas

	TRACTS WITHIN PRIORITY SITES	OTHER TRACTS
Total number of tracts	100	300
Total number of tract owners contacted	90	270
Ownership:		
a. Reside on tract	40	100

*There is ample precedent. The Indiana Natural Areas Registry Program, involving the cooperation of the Indiana Department of Natural Resources and The Nature Conservancy, is funded by a grant from the Lilly Endowment. Likewise, much of the funding for the Illinois Landowner Contact Program has been provided by The Joyce Foundation of Chicago.

b. Individuals not residing on tract	20	70
c. Tracts owned by corporations	30	100
Total	90	270

Attitudes Toward Element:

a. Owner knew of element	45	135
b. Owner managing element for protection	15	45
c. Owner interested in knowing more	20	60
d. Owner's attitude poses threat to element	5	15
e. Not possible to determine	5	15
Total	90	270

Demographics:

a. Owner has owned tract:

1 year or less	35	105
1-5 years	20	60
6-10 years	15	45
11-25 years	10	30
26 + years	10	30
Total	90	270

b. Owner's approximate age (noncorporate tracts):

20-25	5	15
26-35	10	20
36-45	15	40
46-55	10	30
56-65	15	40
66 +	5	25
Total	60	170

Tract Owner's Primary
Need/Desire Regarding Property:

Immediate income	15	45
Long-term investment income	25	75
A place of residence	15	45
Continuity of ownership	10	30
Tax relief	5	15
Productive land	15	45
Structural development	2	6
Recreation	1	3
Serenity	2	6
Total	90	270

189

Tract Owner's Primary Use of Property:		
Crop farming	24	72
Timber	30	90
Ranch	25	75
Industrial	3	9
Residential	3	9
Unimproved	5	15
Total	90	270

The council members felt they were on their way. Next, they sought to match a protection strategy for each tract owner. But even though they were now aware of a range of incentives that owners might find attractive, no member knew the protection options available well enough to know whether they were sufficient. The group elected to research the tools available to see if the options met their needs.

They found that Transylvania conservationists possessed the following options for dealing with nongovernmental owners of significant properties, all of whom had been notified of the significance of their property.

1. Registration.
2. Leases and management agreements.
3. Rights of first refusal.
4. Acquisition of fee title and deferred acquisition of title (bequest or reserved life estate).
5. Less than fee acquisition, or conservation easement.
6. Dedication into the state preserves system.

In addition, the Transylvania Heritage Program coordinated all environmental review requests on behalf of the Department of Natural Resources, and the state possessed good endangered species acts. And most of the state and federal resource agencies were able to set aside areas possessing unusual natural or scientific qualities through their own administrative rules.

They sought to compare the tools, in terms of the primary incentives they offered to landowners, the speed with which they could be applied, the probability each offered for permanent protection or the likelihood of protection in any given year. Research and conversations with conservationists in other states led to the thumbnail sketch in Table 1. For pur-

Table 1—Comparison of the Cost, Speed, Long- and Short-Term Strength, and Incentives Offered by Seven Protection Concepts*

	Cost	Time Required to Apply (workdays)	Probability of Permanent Protection (%)	Strength in Given Year (%)	Uses Per $10,000	Primary Incentives Offered
Notification	$200	1	0	10	50	Information
Registration	$400	2	0	50	20	Recognition, mgt. assist., potential prop. tax relief
Leases/mgt. agreements	$990	3	0	90	10	Slight income, mgt. assist.
Rights of first refusal	$10	2.5	0	10	1,000	Control of present prop. rights
Fee acquisition	·$10,000	20	90	95	1	Income, tax shelter
Conservation easements	$5,000	20	85	95	2	Income, prop. tax reduction, possible residency and partial prop. use
Dedication	$500	5	95	98	20	Confidence of strong prop. tax reduction

*Assumptions relating to these seven concepts follow Table 1.

191

poses of overall comparison, they decided to include notification, even though all owners had been notified.

Assumptions

1. Notification, the cost is that of a single visit and preparation of a site report.
2. Registration, the cost, including production of plaques, brochures, and/or annual visit, is twice that of notification.
3. Leases/management agreements, the cost is $10 per year. The lease is renewable annually for 99 years.
4. Rights of first refusal, the cost is $10 consideration, one time only.
5. Fee acquisition, the cost is $10,000, an arbitrary baseline figure.
6. Conservation easement, the price is 50 percent of fee. Probability of permanent protection is somewhat lower than fee since rights not controlled may pose unforeseen problems.
7. Dedication, cost is only that of administration.

This information suggested a further course of action. They decided to try to calculate how much it would cost to protect, first, the priority tracts and, then, the remaining sites by using a range of protection options. In so doing, they assumed the following:

1. That, given a limited amount of money to spend, they would spend it on the most important places. Thus, they assumed they would try to acquire all 90 privately owned priority tracts whose owners had been notified, and that, by using tax incentives, they could acquire property at 70 percent of fair market value.
2. That the fair market value of those 90 priority tracts is $31,050,000, and the market value of the other 270 privately owned significant tracts whose owners had been notified is $149,400,000.
3. That, as a general rule, they would propose the strongest available tool first, and then work down. So for the priorities they would first acquire property in fee, and failing that they would seek to acquire partial rights through conservation easements.
4. That many sites could be protected in stages, with more than one tool applied over time at the same site. For example, the owner of a tract, once notified, might later agree to sign a voluntary protection agreement. After a year or two of getting to know and like an indi-

vidual representing a conservation group, the owner might allow himself to enter into a formal management agreement and grant a right of first refusal to the conservation group, should he ever decide to sell his property. In time he might do just that, selling at a bargain sale rate. The conservation group could then dedicate their property into a state nature preserve system. That would be six tools at one site over a period of years, and not at all far fetched, providing the owner and the conservationists get to know each other.

5. That everyone agreed to do something. In attempting to compute a cost for using an array of tools to preserve an array of diversity in Transylvania, they came up with the following breakdown.

PRIORITY TRACTS

Total number of tracts	100
Number of tracts negotiators attempted to acquire	90
Number of tracts whose owners agreed	45
Purchase price of the tracts above at 70 percent market value	$10,552,500
Of remaining 45 tracts, number whose owners agreed to conservation easements (the next tool proposed)	15
Purchase price of easements for the 15 tracts, at 50 percent fair market value	$2,587,500
Of remaining 30 tracts, number of tracts whose owners agreed to lease, management agreement, or right of first refusal	15
Cost of the 15 agreements	$150
Of remaining 15 tracts, number whose owners agreed to register property	15
Cost of the 15 registrations	$6,000
Numb r of tracts dedicated into preserve system (the ones acq red through fee and easement)	60
Cost o dedicating these tracts	$30,000

COST FOR PRIORITIES

Acquisition	$10,552,500
Easements	2,587,500
Leases, etc.	150
Registrations	6,000
Dedications	30,000
Total	$13,176,150

SECONDARY TRACTS

Total number of tracts	270

Number of tracts negotiators attempted to acquire in fee	0
Number agreeing to grant easements (of 100 approached)	50
Price of easement at 50 percent fair market value	$13,819,500
Number agreeing to enter into leases, management	
agreements, and rights of first refusal (of 150 approached)	100
Cost of the agreements	$1,000
Number agreeing to register property	
asked first to register	20
those who had already granted easements or entered into	
agreements	100
Cost of 120 registrations	$48,000
Number of dedications (all the easements granted)	50
Cost of dedication	$25,000

COST FOR SECONDARY TRACTS	
Acquisition	0
Easements	$13,819,500
Leases, etc.	1,000
Registration	48,000
Dedication	25,000
Total	$13,893,500

Total Cost of Protecting Priority Sites	$13,176,150
Total Cost of Protecting Secondary Sites	13,893,500
GRAND TOTAL	$27,069,650

The Transylvania Protection Planning Council liked that figure much better than the $180 million required to acquire all private property in fee. They felt that the $27 million, although a mighty sum, was within the realm of possibility, particularly since the group could make a very concrete proposal to the legislature and to private funding sources.

They realized that they had also to persuade public agencies to designate property, but since resource managers for many of the agencies were represented on the council, the outlook appeared sunny.

At this writing the Transylvania Protection Planning Council is hard at work—raising money, negotiating, trying hard, succeeding some, failing some, and learning a lot.

Summary

This chapter modeled in the fictitious state of Transylvania:

1. A process of analyzing heritage program data in order to focus an effort to protect natural ecological diversity.

2. An analytical process that can be used to derive immediate protection priorities.
3. A way to assess the resources available for the job.
4. A comprehensive strategy for employing the various protection tools described previously in this book.
5. A rough comparison of the respective incentives, costs, speed of use, strength, and duration of several protection approaches.

The cost of using thoughtfully a variety of protection techniques to provide varying degrees of protection for a large group of significant property tracts was calculated to be about seven times less than the overall cost of acquiring the same tracts. Still, the protection cost of using the assortment of incentives modeled in an "average" state came out to be a rather stiff $27 million.

Even if the cost seems forbidding, it is important to know the size of the task at hand. A funding proposal begins with the ability to describe the dimensions of the job and the ability to state very clearly why the work described is important. Transylvania conservationists can begin to notify owners, register a large group of tracts, and protect the most important areas through stronger measures—even without vast sums of money—while working to build a durable financial base.

195

RESOURCES

Notes

CHAPTER ONE: THE PRESERVATION OF NATURAL DIVERSITY

1. *The Washington Post,* originally published in *National Review,* reprinted with permission of *The Washington Post* and the author.
2. Much of the information in this chapter has been adapted from materials assembled by John Nutter, director of Heritage Field Operations for The Nature Conservancy, and from the Phase II Document assembled by the Natural Heritage Trust Task Force for presentation to the secretary of the interior and to the president.
3. Norman Meyers, *The Sinking Ark,* (Oxford Pergamon Press, 1979) p. 69.
4. Robert B. Gordon, "The Natural Vegetation of Ohio in Pioneer Days," Bulletin of the Ohio Biological Survey, Vol. III, No. 2, 1969, p. 22.
5. Henry Fairfield Osborne and Harold Elmer Anthony, "Can We Save the Mammals?" *Natural History Magazine,* September/October 1922.
6. *Ibid.*
7. Peter Meyer, "Land Rush—A Survey of America's Land," *Harper's Magazine,* Vol. 258, No. 1544, January 1979, p. 53.
8. Personal conversation with George B. Fell, Executive Secretary, Illinois Nature Preserves Commission.
9. "Developments and Varied Problems Threaten 117 National Landmarks," *The Environmental Journal,* National Parks and Conservation Magazine, March 1979, p. 20.

CHAPTER FOUR: WHY WE NEED MORE WAYS TO PROTECT LAND

1. *Public Land Statistics 1976,* United States Department of the Interior, Bureau of Land Management, U.S. Government Printing Office, Stock No. 024-001-00084-4.
2. Peter Meyer, "Land Rush—A Survey of America's Land," *Harper's Magazine,* Vol. 258, No. 1544, January 1979, pp. 51-52.
3. "The Shrinking Supply of Private Land," *U.S. News and World Report,* February 20, 1978, p. 64.
4. From materials issued by The Heritage Conservation and Recreation Service, U.S. Department of the Interior, Washington, D.C.
5. "The Shrinking Supply of Private Land," p. 64.
6. Meyer, "Land Rush," pp. 51-52.
7. From public remarks by Robert Herbst, Assistant Secretary of the Interior for Fish, Wildlife and Parks; and Meg Maguire, Deputy Assistant Director, Heritage Conservation and Recreation Service.

CHAPTER SIX: REGISTRATION

1. 42 United States Code, 4321 and following.
2. Ohio Revised Code, chapter 1517.
3. Senate Enrolled Act 176 of 1967.
4. Lorraine M. Fleming, *Delaware's Outstanding Natural Areas and Their*

Preservation, (Wilmington, Delaware: William N. Cann, Inc., 1976).

5. Personal conversation with Frank Ugolini, Director, National Natural Landmarks Program.

6. Personal conversation with Mary Ann Young, Director, Natural Areas Program, Georgia Department of Natural Resources.

7. Title 7, U.S. Department of Agriculture Administrative Regulations, Chapter VI, Soil Conservation Service.

8. Indiana Wildlife Habitat Classification Act. Engrossed House Bill 1423.

9. Personal conversation with Ugolini.

10. Nature Conservancy, The. "The Preservation of Natural Diversity: A Survey and Recommendations," prepared for U.S. Department of Interior by The Nature Conservancy, Contract No. CX001-5-0110, 1975, pp. A1-19.

11. Much of the information and all of the statistical material on MCAP was provided by Harry R. Tyler, Director, Maine Critical Areas Program.

12. Maine Revised Statutes, Title 5, Chapter 312.

CHAPTER SEVEN: DESIGNATION OF PUBLIC LANDS

1. Forest Service Manual, 2362.34.

2. *Ibid.*, 2362.44.

3. Lukowski, Wieting et al., *Preserving Our Natural Heritage*, Volume I, *Federal Activities*, prepared for the U.S. Department of the Interior by The Nature Conservancy, 1975, p. 65, U.S. Government Printing Office, Stock No. 024-005-00681.

4. *Ibid.*

5. *Ibid.*, pp. 102-3.

6. Most of the information contained in the Santiago Oak Research Natural Area Case Study was adapted from an unpublished report written and case files provided by John Humke, Director, Midwest Regional Office, The Nature Conservancy, Minneapolis, Minnesota.

CHAPTER EIGHT:
MANAGEMENT AGREEMENTS, LEASES, RIGHTS OF FIRST REFUSAL

1. Personal conversation with Patrick F. Noonan, President, The Nature Conservancy of the United States, shortly after his return from a meeting with British Nature Conservancy officials. It is interesting to note that most of these agreements will expire in the 1980s; and because land values are escalating rapidly, many landowners may now renew them. At present, there are few tax incentives for prospective donors, and the British Nature Conservancy has little money to acquire property. Britain's dilemma again underscores the need for a large and supple system of protection options, including the ability to purchase significant properties.

2. Personal conversation with Timothy Flaherty, Regional Staff Attorney, The Nature Conservancy, Midwest Regional Office, Minneapolis, Minnesota.

3. For a good discussion of the right of preemption, see "The Land Question,"

RTPI Planning Paper No. 4, published in 1974 by The Royal Town Planning Institute, 26 Portland Place, London W1N 4BE, England.

4. Personal conversation with Richard H. Thom, Natural History Section, Missouri Department of Conservation.

CHAPTER NINE: ACQUISITION OF FEE TITLE

1. South Carolina Sessions at Large, 1976, No. 600.

2. An excellent discussion of how to finance a state conservation program appears in the paper "An Analysis of Present Revenue Sources and an Appraisal of New Income Sources," prepared for the Missouri Department of Conservation in 1970 by Arthur W. Betts. The ideas are still instructive.

3. The author owes a major debt for much of the material in this chapter, including the basis for the tax comparisons on pages 101 to 105 and the "Negotiating Tips" section, to an unpublished training notebook titled *Land Preservation Training Program: A Cooperative Venture Between* [what was in 1976] *the Bureau of Outdoor Recreation and The Nature Conservancy*. The material—instructive, sometimes hilarious, and unfortunately now unavailable—was prepared by David E. Morine, Vice President for Land Acquisition, and L. Gregory Low, Executive Vice President, The Nature Conservancy.

4. *Land Conservation and Preservation Techniques*, which was used as a source repeatedly throughout this chapter, was drafted by Timothy Fox, then working with Heritage Conservation and Recreation Service's (HCRS) Mid-Continent Region in Denver.

5. 16 United States Code Annotated, 1523-43.

6. *Land Preservation Training Program*: A Cooperative Venture Between the Bureau of Outdoor Recreation and The Nature Conservancy. Also see *Foundations . . . A Handbook*, prepared by Michael Arabe of HCRS's Mid-Continent Region in Denver. It is available free by writing to HCRS Information Exchange, U.S. Department of the Interior, 440 G Street, NW, Washington, D.C. 20243.

CHAPTER TEN: CONSERVATION EASEMENTS

1. See especially Ross D. Netherton, "Environmental Conservation and Historic Preservation Through Recorded Land Use Agreements," *Real Property Probate and Trust Journal*, Volume 14, Number 3, Fall 1979, especially pp. 542-50. The discussion on the history of easements and their assignability is based on Dr. Netherton's excellent paper.

2. From a report issued by the U.S. General Accounting Office, "The Federal Drive to Acquire Private Lands Should Be Reassessed," December 14, 1979, p. 24.

3. *Scenic Easements in Action*. The proceedings of a conference on scenic easements, sponsored by the University of Wisconsin Law School and held December 16-17, 1966, pp. 11-12.

4. Harold C. Jordahl, Jr., "Conservation and Scenic Easements: An Experience Resume," from *Land Economics*, Volume 39, No. 4, November 1963, published quarterly by the University of Wisconsin.
5. *Ibid.*, pp. 359-62.
6. Steve Taff, "The Wisconsin Department of Natural Resource's Conservation Easement Program: 1961-1973," an unpublished paper written in connection with the University of Wisconsin Law School, Spring 1974.
7. Ralph J. Brown and Jerome M. Schmitz, "Appraising Wetlands Easements," in *The Appraisal Journal*, April 1978.
8. From *Land Conservation and Preservation Techniques*, Heritage Conservation and Recreation Service, U.S. Department of the Interior, text prepared by Timothy Fox, p. 27.
9. Taff, "Conservation Easement Program," p. 20.
10. Rebecca Warren, "Local Land Conservation in Maine," edited and published by the Maine Coast Heritage Trust, case study No. 4, 1978.
11. David C. Baumgartner and Ronald I. Beazley, "Taxation of Forest and Associated Land in Illinois," U.S.D.A. Forest Service Research Paper NC-165, North Central Forest Experiment Station, St. Paul, Minnesota, 1979.
12. Colorado Revised Statutes, 1973, section 38-30.5-104(2).
13. Written by Michael G. DiNunzio and Thomas C. Field, Gansevoort, New York, June 1980.

CHAPTER ELEVEN: DEDICATION

1. Ohio Revised Code, section 1517.06.
2. South Carolina Sessions at Large, 1976, No. 600.
3. Phillip M. Hoose, "Leaving Water in Western Streams," *The Nature Conservancy News*, Volume 29, Number 1, January/February 1979.

CHAPTER TWELVE: LOBBYING

1. The structure of this chapter is based on unpublished descriptions of the legislative process, which were drafted by Rick Fortenberry during his tenure as the director of the Mississippi field office of The Nature Conservancy.

CHAPTER THIRTEEN: ENVIRONMENTAL REVIEW

1. From Natural Resources Defense Council Files.
2. From The Tenth Annual Report of the Council on Environmental Quality, December 1979, pp. 565-602.
3. Linda McMahan, "Legal Protection for Rare Plant Species," *American University Law Review*, May 1980.
4. From the Office on Endangered Species, personal conversation.
5. Remarks made May 19, 1978, by Hugh A. Barker, President, Public Service of Indiana.
6. J.C. Collins et al., "Rare Vascular Plants of Tennessee," *Journal of the Tennessee Academy of Sciences*, 1976.

Key Contacts

The people listed below have thought about and experimented with landowner contact programs. They are good sources of information.

CHAPTER FIVE: NOTIFICATION

Jerry Paulson, Director
Illinois Landowner Contact Program
Natural Land Institute
320 South Third Street
Rockford, Illinois 61108

Lydia Sargent Meyer, Field Representative
Illinois Landowner Contact Program
Natural Land Institute
320 South Third Street
Rockford, Illinois 61108
The passages attributed to Lydia in the text
are excerpted from "Illinois Landowner
Contact Program: A Personal Point of View,"
paper written September 15, 1979, by Lydia
Meyer.

Hank Tyler, Director
Maine Critical Areas Program
185 State Street
Augusta, Maine 04335

Charles Roe, Coordinator
North Carolina Natural Heritage Program
Division of State Parks
Department of Natural and Economic
Resources
Box 27687
Raleigh, North Carolina 27611

CHAPTER EIGHT:
MANAGEMENT AGREEMENTS, LEASES, RIGHTS OF FIRST REFUSAL

Leases:

Mike Dennis, General Counsel
The Nature Conservancy
1800 North Kent Street
Arlington, Virginia 22209

Timothy Flaherty, Staff Attorney
The Nature Conservancy
Midwest Regional Office
328 East Hennepin Avenue
Minneapolis, Minnesota 55414

Management agreements:

Mike Green, Director
Florida Field Office
The Nature Conservancy
935 Orange Avenue, Suite B
Winter Park, Florida 32789

Nature Conservancy of England
19-20 Belgrave Square
London SW1X 8PY
England

Richard H. Thom, Natural Areas Coordinator
Department of Conservation
2901 Ten Mile Drive
P.O. Box 180
Jefferson City, Missouri 65101

Rights of first refusal:

Tom Massengale, Director
The Nature Conservancy
North Carolina Field Office
P.O. Box 805
Chapel Hill, North Carolina 27514

William Quisenberry, Director
Mississippi Wildlife Heritage Program
P.O. Box 451
Jackson, Mississippi 39205

CHAPTER NINE: ACQUISITION OF FEE TITLE

The Nature Conservancy's national office is located at 1800 North Kent Street, Arlington, Virginia 22209. Following is a list of its state and regional field offices.

Eastern Regional Office
Bradford C. Northrup, Vice President
294 Washington Street, Room 850
Boston, **Massachusetts** 02108
(617) 542-1908

Midwest Regional Office
John W. Humke, Vice President
328 East Hennepin Avenue
Minneapolis, **Minnesota** 55414
(612) 379-2134

Southeast Regional Office
Charles L. Scott, Director
1800 North Kent Street
Arlington, **Virginia** 22209
(703) 841-5312

Western Regional Office
Henry Little, Vice President
425 Bush Street, 5th floor
San Francisco, **California** 94108
(415) 989-3056

New York Development Office
William B. Carlin, Director
36 West 44th Street, Room 307
New York, **New York** 10036
(212) 869-9532

Northwest Field Office
Spencer Beebe, Director
1234 N.W. 25th
Portland, **Oregon** 97210
(503) 228-9561

California Field Office
Peter Seligmann, Director
425 Bush Street, 5th floor
San Francisco, **California** 94108
(415) 989-3056

Colorado Field Office
Chip Collins, Director
820 Sixteenth Street, Suite 420
Denver, **Colorado** 80202
(303) 623-8088

Florida Field Office
Michael L. Green, Director
935 Orange Avenue, Suite B
Winter Park, **Florida** 32789

Georgia Field Office
Riesley R. Jones, Director
7564 Lowilla Lane
Lithonia, **Georgia** 30058
(404) 482-4650

Great Plains Field Office
John Flicker, Director
328 East Hennepin Avenue
Minneapolis, **Minnesota** 55414
(612) 379-2134

Illinois Field Office
Ralph Brown, Director
666 N. Lake Shore Drive
Suite 1919
Chicago, **Illinois** 60611
(312) 787-1791

Indiana Field Office
Marion Jackson, Director
Route 1, Box 155
Nashville, **Indiana** 47448
(812) 988-7547

Maryland/Delaware Field Office
Steve Hamblin, Director
Chevy Chase Center Office Bldg.
35 Wisconsin Circle, Suite 304
Chevy Chase, **Maryland** 20015
(301) 656-8673

Michigan Field Office
Suite F, 531 Clippert Street
Lansing, **Michigan** 48912
(517) 332-1741

Minnesota Field Office
Geoffrey S. Barnard, Director
328 East Hennepin Avenue
Minneapolis, **Minnesota** 55414
(612) 379-2134

Montana/Wyoming Office
Robert J. Kiesling, Director
P.O. Box 258
The Diamond Block
Helena, **Montana** 59601
(406) 443-0303

New Mexico Field Office
William C. Briggs, Director
610 Gold Avenue, S.W.
P.O. Box 1846
Albuquerque, **New Mexico** 87103
(505) 242-2015

North Carolina Field Office
Thomas Massengale, Director
P.O. Box 805
Chapel Hill, **North Carolina** 27514
(919) 967-1406

Ohio Field Office
David Younkman, Director
1504 West 1st Avenue
Columbus, **Ohio** 43212
(614) 486-4194

Oregon Field Office
Al Edelman, Director
1234 N.W. 25th
Portland, **Oregon** 97210
(503) 228-9561

Pennsylvania/New Jersey Office
R.T. Cook, Director
1218 Chestnut Street, Suite 801
Philadelphia, **Pennsylvania** 19107
(215) 925-1065

South Carolina Field Office
LaBruce Alexander, Director
P.O. Box 5475
Columbia, **South Carolina** 29250
(803) 254-9049

Tennessee Field Office
Catherine Day Lohman, Director
1720 West End Avenue, Suite 600
Nashville, **Tennessee** 37203
(615) 320-1465

Texas Field Office
R. Scott Spann, Director
201 N. St. Mary's
Suite 618
San Antonio, **Texas** 78205
(512) 222-9665

Vermont Field Office
Robert J. Klein, Director
7 Main Street
Montpelier, **Vermont** 05602
(802) 229-4425

Virginia Field Office
William M. Cole, Director
415 Park Street
Charlottesville, **Virginia** 22901
(804) 295-6106

Washington Field Office
Elliot Marks, Director
618 Smith Tower
Seattle, **Washington** 98104
(206) 624-9623

West Virginia Field Office
Ed Maguire, Director
1100 Quarrier Street, Room 215
Charleston, **West Virginia** 25301
(304) 345-4350

Wisconsin Field Office
Russell Van Herik, Director
1922 University Avenue
Madison, **Wisconsin** 53705
(608) 233-9721

The Heritage Conservation and Recreation Service administers the Land and Water Conservation Fund. For a list of regional offices, write to HCRS at U.S. Department of the Interior, 440 G Street, NW, Washington, D.C. 20243.

State Liaison Officers approve the eligiblity of acquisition projects for state Land and Water Conservation Fund monies. Following is a list of State Liaison Officers, current through 1979.

John W. Hodnett, Commissioner
Department of Conservation
and Natural Resources
Administrative Building
Montgomery, **Alabama** 36104
(205) 832-6361

Terry McWilliams, Director
Division of Parks
323 East Fourth Avenue
Anchorage, **Alaska** 99501
(907) 274-4676

Tom Cablk
Office of the Governor
Government of American Samoa
Pago Pago, Tutuila
American Samoa 96799

Roland H. Sharer
Outdoor Recreation
Coordinating Commission
4433 North 19th Avenue, Suite 203
Phoenix, **Arizona** 85015
(602) 271-5013

Ronald Copeland, Director
Arkansas Department of Local Services
First National Bank Building, Suite 900
Little Rock, **Arkansas** 72201
(501) 371-2671

Herbert Rhodes, Director
Department of Parks and Recreation
P.O. Box 2390
Sacramento, **California** 95811
(916) 445-2358

George T. O'Malley, Jr., Director
Division of Parks and Outdoor Recreation
Department of Natural Resources
1313 Sherman Street, Room 604
Denver, **Colorado** 80203
(303) 892-3437

Stanley J. Pac, Commissioner
Department of Environmental Protection
117 State Office Building
Hartford, **Connecticut** 06115
(203) 566-2110

Austin P. Olney, Assistant Secretary
Department of Natural Resources
and Environmental Control
Edward Tatnall Building
Dover, **Delaware** 19901
(302) 678-4403

William H. Rumsey, Director
D.C. Recreation Department
3149 16th Street, NW
Washington, **D.C.** 20010
(202) 628-6000

Ney C. Landrum, Director
Division of Recreation and Parks
Department of Natural Resources
Crown Building
202 Blount Street

Tallahassee, **Florida** 32304
(904) 488-6131

Joe D. Tanner, Commissioner
State Department of Natural Resources
270 Washington Street, S.W.
Atlanta, **Georgia** 30334
(404) 656-3500

Robert G.P. Cruz, Director
Department of Parks and Recreation
P.O. Box 682
Agana, **Guam** 96910

Hideto Kono, Director
Department of Planning
and Economic Development
P.O. Box 2359
Honolulu, **Hawaii** 96804
(808) 548-6914

Dale R. Christiansen, Director
Department of Parks and Recreation
Statehouse
Boise, **Idaho** 83720
(208) 384-2154

Dr. David Kenney, Director
Department of Conservation
602 State Office Building
Springfield, **Illinois** 62706
(217) 782-6302

Joseph D. Cloud, Director
Department of Natural Resources
608 State Office Building
Indianapolis, **Indiana** 46204
(317) 633-6344

Fred A. Priewert, Director
State Conservation Commission
State Office Building
300 4th Street
Des Moines, **Iowa** 50319
(515) 281-5384

Lynn Burris, Jr., Director
State Park and Resources Authority
P.O. Box 977
Topeka, **Kansas** 66601
(913) 296-2281

Bruce Montgomery, Commissioner
State Department of Parks
Capitol Plaza Tower, 10th Floor
Frankfort, **Kentucky** 40601
(502) 564-4260

Sandra S. Thompson, Secretary
Department of Culture,
Recreation and Tourism
P.O. Box Drawer 1111
625 North 4th Street
Baton Rouge, **Louisiana** 70821
(504) 389-5761

Herbert W. Hartman, Director
Bureau of Parks & Recreation
Department of Conservation
State Office Building
Augusta, **Maine** 04333
(207) 289-3821

Louis N. Phipps, Deputy Secretary
Department of Natural Resources
Tawes State Office Building
Annapolis, **Maryland** 21401
(301) 267-5043

Dr. Evelyn Murphy, Secretary
Department of Environmental Affairs
State Office Building Government Center
100 Cambridge Street
Boston, **Massachusetts** 02202
(617) 727-3163

Orie Scherschligt, Deputy Director
Department of Natural Resources
Stevens T. Mason Building
Lansing, **Michigan** 48926
(517) 373-2682

Barbara Clark,
Assistant Commissioner for Planning
Department of Natural Resources
301 Centennial Building
658 Cedar Street
St. Paul, **Minnesota** 55101
(612) 296-2549

Rae Sanders, Outdoor Recreation Director
Mississippi Park System
Robert E. Lee Building
Jackson, **Mississippi** 39201
(601) 354-6338

Fred A. Lafser, Director
Division of Parks and Recreation
Department of Natural Resources
Box 176
Jefferson City, **Missouri** 65101
(314) 635-3332

Ronnie G. Holliday, Administrator
Recreation and Parks Division
Department of Fish and Game
Mitchell Building
Helena, **Montana** 59601
(406) 449-3066

Eugene T. Mahoney, Director
Game and Parks Commission
2200 North 33rd Street
P.O. Box 30370
Lincoln, **Nebraska** 68503
(402) 464-0641

Norman Hall, Director
Department of Conservation
and Natural Resources
Nye Building, Room 214
Carson City, **Nevada** 89701
(702) 885-4360

George Gilman, Commissioner
Department of Resources
and Economic Development
State House Annex
Concord, **New Hampshire** 03301
(603) 271-2411

Rocco D. Ricci, Commissioner (Acting)
Department of Environmental Protection
John Fitch Plaza
P.O. Box 1390
Trenton, **New Jersey** 08625
(609) 292-2886

Leila Andrews, State Planning Officer
505 Don Gaspar Avenue
Santa Fe, **New Mexico** 87503
(505) 827-2073

Orin Lehman, Commissioner
Office of Parks and Recreation
South Swan Street Building
Albany, **New York** 12223
(518) 474-0443

Howard N. Lee, Secretary
Department of Natural
and Economic Resources
P.O. Box 27687
Raleigh, **North Carolina** 27611
(919) 733-4984

Tim Mueller, Director
Parks and Recreation Department
State Park Service
Box 139, Rural Route 2
Mandan, **North Dakota** 58554
(701) 663-3943

Robert W. Teater, Director
Department of Natural Resources
1952 Belcher Drive
Fountain Square
Columbus, **Ohio** 43224
(614) 466-3770

Abe L. Hesser, Executive Director
Tourism and Recreation Department
500 Will Rogers Memorial Building
Oklahoma City, **Oklahoma** 73105
(405) 521-2413

David G. Talbot, State Parks Superintendent
555 Trade Street, SE
Salem, **Oregon** 97310
(503) 378-6305

William H. Wilcox,
Secretary of Community Affairs
P.O. Box 155
Harrisburg, **Pennsylvania** 17120
(717) 787-7160

Jose C. Barbosa Muniz, Administrator
Public Parks and Recreation Administration
P.O. Box 3207
San Juan, **Puerto Rico** 00904
(809) 725-1966

William W. Harsch, Director
Department of Natural Resources
Veterans' Memorial Building
83 Park Street
Providence, **Rhode Island** 02903
(401) 277-2771

William B. Depass, Jr., Director
Bureau of Outdoor Recreation
Department of Parks, Recreation and Tourism
Edgar A. Brown Building, Suite 113
1205 Pendleton Street
Columbia, **South Carolina** 29202
(803) 758-7705

Jack Merwin, Secretary
Department of Game, Fish and Parks
State Office Building # 1
Pierre, **South Dakota** 57501
(605) 224-3387

B.R. Allison, Commissioner
Department of Conservation
2611 West End Avenue
Nashville, **Tennessee** 37203
(615) 741-1061

Pearce Johnson, Chairman
Parks and Wildlife Commission
4200 Smith School Road
Austin, **Texas** 78744
(512) 475-2087

Gordon E. Harmston, Executive Director
Department of Natural Resources
438 State Capitol Building
Salt Lake City, **Utah** 84114
(801) 533-5356

Edward J. Koenemann, Director
Planning Division
Agency of Environmental Conservation
Statehouse
Montpelier, **Vermont** 05602
(802) 828-5691

Virdin C. Brown, Commissioner
Department of Conservation
and Cultural Affairs
P.O. Box 578
Charlotte Amalie
St. Thomas, **Virgin Islands** 00801
(809) 774-3320

Rob R. Blackmore, Director
Commission of Outdoor Recreation
803 East Broad Street
Richmond, **Virginia** 23219
(804) 786-2036

Robert L. Wilder, Administrator
Interagency Committee for
Outdoor Recreation
4800 Capitol Boulevard
Tumwater, **Washington** 98504
(206) 753-7140

Michael Wenger, State Liaison Officer
Office of Federal-State Relations
State Capitol Building, Room 144-WW
Charleston, **West Virginia** 25305
(304) 345-3361

Paul Guthrie, Director
Office of Intergovernmental Programs
Department of Natural Resources
Box 450
Madison, **Wisconsin** 53701
(608) 266-2121

Paul H. Westedt, Director
Wyoming Recreation Commission
604 East 25th Street
Cheyenne, **Wyoming** 82002
(307) 777-7695

CHAPTER TEN: CONSERVATION EASEMENTS

Legal experts:

Glen Tiedt
HCRS - USDI
P.O. Box 25387
Denver Federal Center
Denver, **Colorado** 80225

Russell Brenneman
60 Washington Street, Suite 1212
Hartford, **Connecticut** 06106

Ross Netherton
Office of Research
HRS 41
Federal Highway Administration
Washington, **D.C.** 20590

Kingsbury Browne
Hill & Barlow
225 Franklin Street
Boston, **Massachusetts** 02110

Harold Jordahl, Professor
Natural Resources & Environmental Studies
112C Music Hall
University of Wisconsin
Madison, **Wisconsin** 53706

Experienced practitioners:

Ben Emory, Executive Director
Maine Coast Heritage Trust
P.O. Box 426
Northeast Harbor, **Maine** 04662

Whitney Beals and Ron Killian
Regional Land Stewards
The Nature Conservancy
294 Washington Street, Room 851
Boston, **Massachusetts** 02108

John R. Flicker, Field Representative
Midwestern Regional Office
328 East Hennepin Avenue
Minneapolis, **Minnesota** 55414

Mike Dennis, General Counsel
The Nature Conservancy
1800 North Kent Street
Arlington, **Virginia** 22209

CHAPTER ELEVEN: DEDICATION

Officials in charge of agencies that administer nature preserves systems

Harold Grimmett, Executive Director
Arkansas Natural Heritage Commission
Continental Building, Suite 500
Maine and Marham
Little Rock, **Arkansas** 72201

J. Patrick Redden, Director
Office of Heritage Planning and Research
Department of Natural Resources and
Environmental Control
The Edward Tatnall Building
P.O. Box 1401
Dover, **Delaware** 19901

George Fell, Executive Secretary
Illinois Nature Preserves Commission
320 South Third Street
Rockford, **Illinois** 61108

John Bacone, Director
Indiana Division of Nature Preserves
State Office Building
Indianapolis, **Indiana** 46204

Dorothy Baringer, Chairperson
Iowa State Preserves Advisory Board
1405 Pleasant Drive
West Des Moines, **Iowa** 50265

Lynn Barris, Jr., Director
Kansas State Park and Resources Authority
503 Kansas Avenue
P.O. Box 997
Topeka, **Kansas** 66601

John Rickert, Chairman
Kentucky Nature Preserves Commission
122 North Main
Elizabethtown, **Kentucky** 42701

William Quisenberry, Director
Mississippi Wildlife Heritage Committee
P.O. Box 451
Jackson, **Mississippi** 39205

Dr. Robert M. Horne, Director
North Dakota Parks
and Recreation Department
R.D. 2, Box 139
Mandan, **North Dakota** 58554

Richard E. Moseley, Jr., Chief
Division of Natural Areas and Preserves
Department of Natural Resources
Fountain Square
Columbus, **Ohio** 43224

Jack Mills, Chairman
Oregon Natural Heritage Advisory Council
Division of State Lands
1445 State Street
Salem, **Oregon** 97310

Dr. James A. Timmerman, Jr.,
Executive Director
South Carolina Wildlife and Marine
Preserves Department
Building "D", Dutch Plaza, Box 167
Columbia, **South Carolina** 29202

Selected Bibliography

CHAPTER ONE: THE PRESERVATION OF NATURAL DIVERSITY

Agarwal, Anil. "Eye of Newt and Toe of Frog" [traditional natural medicines]. *New Scientist*, November 2, 1978.

Buckley, James. "In Defense of Snail Darters." *Washington Post*, September 4, 1979.

Eckholm, Erik. *Disappearing Species: The Social Challenge.* Washington, D.C.: Worldwatch Papers, July 1978.

Roush, G. Jon. "Why Save Diversity?" *The Nature Conservancy News*, Winter 1977.

Thompson, Peter A. "Factors Involved in the Selection of Plant Resources for Conservation as Seed in Gene Banks." *Biological Conservation*, 1976.

CHAPTER TWO: STATE NATURAL HERITAGE INVENTORIES

Jenkins, Robert E. "Maintenance of Natural Diversity: Approach and Recommendations." Forty-first North American Wildlife and Natural Resources Conference, Washington, March 21-25, 1976.

Nature Conservancy, The. "North Carolina Natural Heritage Program Report." North Carolina Department of Natural and Economic Resources, May 31, 1978.

CHAPTER THREE: ORGANIZING A STATEWIDE PROTECTION PLAN

Nature Conservancy, The. "North Carolina Natural Heritage Program Report." North Carolina Department of Natural and Economic Resources, 1979.

CHAPTER FOUR: WHY WE NEED MORE WAYS TO PROTECT LAND

General Accounting Office, U.S. "The Federal Drive to Acquire Private Lands Should be Reassessed." December 14, 1979.

Nature Conservancy, The. *The Preservation of Natural Diversity: A Survey and Recommendations.* Prepared for the Department of the Interior, 1975.

CHAPTER FIVE: NOTIFICATION

Paulson, Gerald. "Landowner Contact Program," from the preliminary draft of *State Natural Areas Plan.* Illinois Department of Conservation, in cooperation with the Illinois Nature Preserves Commission and the Endangered Species Protection Board, 1979.

CHAPTER SIX: REGISTRATION

Federal Register. "Interim Regulations of the National Natural Landmarks Program." Section entitled "Regulation," 1212.6, Volume 44, No. 225, pp. 66599-602, November 20, 1979.

Heritage Conservation and Recreation Service, U.S. Department of the Interior. "The National Natural Landmarks Program." Department of Interior Document No. INT 3983-79, May 19, 1979.

Klein, Robert. "Long Term Protection of Maine's Critical Areas." A report prepared for Maine's Critical Areas Program, State Planning Office, by The Nature Conservancy, 1980.

Meyer, Lydia Sargent. "Illinois Landowner Contact Program: A Personal Point of View." September 1979.

Witherill, Donald T. "The Effects of Critical Area Designation on Title Transfers of Land." May 15, 1979, an unpublished paper, available from Maine Critical Areas Program, 185 State Street, Augusta, Maine 04333.

CHAPTER SEVEN: DESIGNATION OF PUBLIC LANDS

Dyrness, C.T., et al. eds. "Research Natural Area Needs in the Pacific Northwest; A Contribution to Land-Use Planning. Report on Natural Areas Needs Workshop, November 29-December 1, 1973, Portland, Oregon." Pacific NW Forest and Range Experiment Station, U.S.D.A.-Forest Service, 1975.

Franklin, Jerry F.; Jenkins, Robert E.; and Romancier, Robert M. "Research Natural Areas: Contributors to Environmental Quality Programs." *Journal of Environmental Quality*, 1972.

Nature Conservancy, The. *Preserving Our Natural Heritage*, Volume I, *Federal Activities*. Washington, D.C.: U.S. Government Printing Office, October 31, 1975.

Nature Conservancy, The. *Preserving Our Natural Heritage*, Volume II, *State Activities*. Washington, D.C.: U.S. Government Printing Office, July 31, 1976.

CHAPTER EIGHT:
MANAGEMENT AGREEMENTS, LEASES, RIGHTS OF FIRST REFUSAL

Royal Town Planning Institute, The. "The Land Question." RTPI Planning Paper Number 4, published in 1974 by The Royal Town Planning Institute, London W1N 4BE.

CHAPTER NINE: ACQUISITION OF FEE TITLE

Betts, Arthur W. "An Analysis of Present Revenue Sources and an Appraisal of New Income Sources." Prepared for the Missouri Department of Conservation, 1970.

Fox, Timothy. *Land Conservation and Preservation Techniques*. Prepared for Heritage Conservation and Recreation Service's (HCRS) Mid-Continent Region in Denver, Colorado, 1978.

Noonan, Patrick F. "The Virginia Coast Reserve: Acquisition Strategies for Coastal Zone Preservation." *Coastal Zone Management Journal*, 1977.

Stover, Emily, ed. *Protecting Nature's Estate: Techniques for Saving Land*. U.S. Bureau of Outdoor Recreation (now HCRS), December 1975.

CHAPTER TEN: CONSERVATION EASEMENTS

Brenneman, Russell L. *Private Approaches to the Preservation of Public Land*. Waterford, Connecticut: The Conservation and Research Foundation, 1967.

Daugherty, Arthur B. "Open Space Preservation—Federal Tax Policies Encouraging Donation of Conservation Easements." U.S. Department of Agriculture, Economics, Statistics, and Cooperatives Service, 1978.

Di Nunzio, Michael G., and Field, Thomas C. "Conservation Easement Resource Evaluation Procedures for The Nature Conservancy." Gansevoort, New York, June 1980.

Montana Land Reliance. "Conservation Law Seminar—Conservation Easements and Related Charitable Conveyances." Montana Land Reliance, July 20, 1979.

Netherton, Ross D. "Environmental Conservation and Historic Preservation Through Recorded Land-Use Agreements." *Real Property, Probate and Trust Journal*, Volume 14, Fall 1979.

CHAPTER ELEVEN: DEDICATION

Nature Conservancy, The. *The Preservation of Natural Diversity: A Survey and Recommendations.* Prepared for the Department of the Interior, 1975.

CHAPTER TWELVE: LOBBYING

League of Women Voters. "Know Your State." League of Women Voters, U.S. Education Fund, publication No. 137, 1974.

Redman, Eric. *The Dance of Legislation.* North Hollywood: Symbols and Signs, 1973.

Wilson, Vincent. *Book of the States.* Brookerville, Maryland: American Historical Research Association, 1972.

CHAPTER THIRTEEN: ENVIRONMENTAL REVIEW

McMahan, Linda. "Legal Protection for Rare Plant Species." *American University Law Review*, May 1980.

National Environmental Policy Act, 42 United States Code, 4321 and following.

Natural Resources Defense Council, Inc. *Land Use Controls in New York State.* New York: The Dial Press/James Wade, 1975.

Natural Resources Defense Council, Inc. *Land Use Controls in the United States.* New York: The Dial Press/James Wade, 1975.

Index

Also available from Island Press
Star Route 1, Box 38, Covelo, CA 95428

Headwaters: Tales of the Wilderness, by Ash, Russell, Doog, and Del Rio; Preface by Edward Abbey. Photographs and illustrations. $6.00.

Four bridge-playing buddies tackle the wilderness—they go in separately, meet on top of a rock, and come out talking. These four are as different as the suits in their deck of cards, as ragged as a three-day beard, and as eager as sparks.

Wellspring: A Story from the Deep Country, by Barbara Dean. Illustrations. $6.00.

A woman's life in tandem with nature—the honest, often beautiful telling of one woman's life in a rugged setting, both geographically and emotionally. This book is at once a pioneer's journal and a record of our times.

The Christmas Coat, by Ron Jones. Illustrations. $4.00.

A contemporary fable of a mysterious Christmas gift and a father's search for the sender, which takes him to his wife, his son, and his memories of big band and ballroom days.

An Everyday History of Somewhere, by Ray Raphael; illustrations by Mark Livingston. $9.00.

"The true story of Indians, Deer, Homesteaders, potatoes, loggers, trees, fishermen, salmon, and other living things in the backwoods of northern California." A fresh, inviting look into all of our pasts, from the perspective of everyday lives.

The Search for Goodbye-to-Rains, by Paul McHugh. $7.50.

Steve Getane takes to the road in an American odyssey that is part fantasy and part real—a haphazard pursuit that includes Faulkner's Mississippi, the rarefied New Mexico air, and a motorcycle named Frank. "A rich, resonant novel of the interior world. Overtones of Whitman, Kerouac."—Robert Anton Wilson

Please send $1.00 for postage and handling with all orders. A catalog of current and forthcoming Island Press titles also is available.

Design by Philip Speegle
Editing by Barbara Youngblood
Titles set in Novarese Book by Community Type and Design, Fairfax, California
Text set in Baskerville by digi-type, inc., Santa Rosa, California
Printed by Banta Company, Curtis Reed Plaza, Menasha, Wisconsin.